Contemporary English Criticism
Theory and Practice

Amar Nath Dwivedi

ATLANTIC
PUBLISHERS & DISTRIBUTORS (P) LTD

Published by
ATLANTIC
PUBLISHERS & DISTRIBUTORS (P) LTD
7/22, Ansari Road, Darya Ganj, New Delhi-110002
Phones : +91-11-40775252, 40775214, 23273880, 23275880
Fax : +91-11-23285873
Web : www.atlanticbooks.com
E-mail : orders@atlanticbooks.com

Branch Office: Chennai
Phones : +91-44-48531784, 28291383
E-mail : chennai@atlanticbooks.com

Printed & bound in India by Atlantic Print Services

For

Kartikeya

Vedansh

with love and blessings

Preface

This is a compilation of my critical essays written from time to time to meet the exigencies of national seminars and conferences held by the English Departments of various universities and colleges. Sometimes, journals and magazines also made demands of papers, and I readily responded to them with a positive note. Here, I have put together only those essays and papers which have a direct bearing on the subject of my study, that is, Contemporary English Criticism—Theory and Practice. This clearly implies that I have followed the process of selection and rejection while compiling this critical anthology. I have written many more essays and papers, but selected only those which do not fall beyond the purview of my study. This is a rigorous process, since one has to keep in mind what is 'contemporary' in English criticism and also what is 'theory in practice' and what is 'practice in theory'.

A brief analysis of the essays and papers included in this anthology will clarify my point. The book includes twelve chapters. The first one deals with the subaltern writings in English which forcefully raised the voice of the voiceless; of the suppressed and exploited classes; of the SC and ST classes; and of the lower sections of society. Like these classes, women are also a marginalized and oppressed class, and they have been studied through the writings of various authors, such as Kamala Markandaya, Nayantara Sahgal, Shashi Deshpande, Githa Hariharan, Arundhati Roy, and Manju Kapur among Indians; Bharati Mukherjee, a diasporic author; and Toni Morrison, an Afro-American writer. For a study of the condition of SCs, STs, and Dalits, I have gone to Munshi Premchand's *Godan*

(1957 English ed.), Mulk Raj Anand's *Untouchable* (1935), and Arundhati Roy's *The God of Small Things* (1997). This essay concludes by pointing out that the voice of the subaltern is now heard with honor and interest, on almost every platform of literary discussions and debates.

The second one discusses the diasporic writing in English. The term 'diaspora' denotes a diversion or dispersal of a group of people to a foreign land, away from their homelands. Clearly, the whole discussion veers round the idea of the Indian diasporic writing in English. Diasporic writings may also be called 'expatriate writings' or 'immigrant writings'. All such writings are characterized by a sense of isolation and nostalgia, rootlessness and homelessness. The main theorists of Diaspora are Edward Said, Homi K. Bhabha, and Gayatri Chakravorty Spivak. These theorists are also the theorists of 'Colonialism' and 'Postcolonialism'. The names of Frantz Fanon, Bill Ashcraft, Gareth Griffiths, and Helen Tiffin may be added to the latter list. Since the earliest times, Indians have been going abroad and settling down there, temporarily or permanently. Some of these Indians are creatively talented and made use of their talent in producing works of quality. These writers can be divided into two groups—those of older generation and those of younger generation. The list of such writers is long. These writers are now living in countries like Britain, America, Canada, Germany, Australia, and the West Indies. Their literary contribution deserves attention and appreciation.

The third essay/paper is on new English literatures of the colonized. Naturally, the focus is on new English literatures being written by the inhabitants of the erstwhile colonized countries whose liberation from one or the other imperial power of the West makes all the difference. These writers are now writing with a changed attitude, recasting their history and inheritance, and paying back to the old masters in their own coin. This changed attitude may be called a subversion or decolonization of language, history, education, and culture. In this paper, it is shown how this subversion or decolonization is effected in new literatures of Africa/South Africa, the West Indies, and India in a major way, and in those of Australia, New Zealand, and Canada in a limited way. For a study of new literatures, *The Empire Writes Back* (1989) by Bill Ashcroft, Gareth Griffiths and Helen Tiffin, *Nation and Narration* (1990) by Homi K. Bhabha, and earlier than these *The Wretched of the Earth* (1961) by Frantz Fanon are quite useful.

The fourth essay/paper takes up a twentieth-century critic, T.S. Eliot (1988-1965), for studying his criticism *vis-à-vis* the critical formulations of the Great English Romantics. It makes a comparative study of Eliot and the Great Romantics—William Wordsworth (1770-1850), S.T. Coleridge (1972-1834), P.B. Shelley (1792-1822), and John Keats (1795-1821). Though Eliot pronounced to be 'a classicist in literature', he shows the traces of Romanticism in his early poetry, notably in his *Poems Written in Early Youth* (1967) and *The Love Song of J. Alfred Prufrock* (1915). I have no hesitation in revealing that I read a Ph.D. thesis in English from the Lucknow University on "Romantic Strains in T.S. Eliot's Poetry" about two decades ago, and that I was impressed with it. Eliot's well-known concept of classicism as embedded in his 'impersonal theory of poetry', 'objective correlative', 'unification of sensibility', 'auditory imagination', finds parallels in the great Romantic critics. They may differ on the question of the use of poetic diction, on objectivity or subjectivity of poetry, or on the application of imagination, but on vital issues of criticism they are, more or less, identical. Eliot and the Great Romantics also share the view that poetry has a social function.

The fifth essay/paper is devoted to a discussion of Native Modernity in Indian English Fiction. For one thing, Native Modernity is not essentially different from Modernity or Modernism. The term 'Native' indicates 'Modernity' in the Indian context, and suggests its own brand, its own peculiar traits, and its indigenous growth. It does not denote, in any way, westernization of our development, customs, and manners. Of course, native modernity aims at development through the promotion of cottage industries and indigenous crafts. This paper attempts to study one or two texts of such modernist authors as Raja Rao, Arun Joshi, Anita Desai, Shashi Deshpande, Arundhati Roy and Aravind Adiga. These authors are models of native modernity.

The sixth essay/paper moves a step ahead and considers Postmodernism in Indian English Fiction. It undertakes to study Salman Rushdie's *Midnight's Children* (1981), Arundhati Roy's *The God of Small Things* (1997), and Aravind Adiga's *The White Tiger* (2008) as samples of postmodernist texts. Some of the prominent issues and challenges of Postmodernism are lack of the center/centrality, birth of chaos and disorder, want of faith and conviction, certainty of the uncertainty, indeterminism, and virtual reality. The texts taken up for study elucidate these issues and challenges.

The seventh essay/paper examines Magic Realism in Rushdie's *The Enchantress of Florence* (2008). 'Magic Realism' (or 'Magical Realism') is a narrative mode that offers a way to "discuss alternative approaches to reality to that of Western philosophy, expressed in many postcolonial and non-Western works of contemporary fiction" (Maggie Ann Bowers, 2004: 1). As a narrative mode of art and literature, it strives to reach beyond the confines of Realism and draws upon the resources of fable, folktale, and myth. Magic Realism is largely found in contemporary fiction of such non-Western writers as Gabriel Garcia Marquez, Salman Rushdie, Chitra Banerjee Divakaruni, and Rohinton Mistry. This essay/paper examines Rushdie's *The Enchantress of Florence* as a remarkable piece of Magic Realism.

The eighth essay/paper dwells on Myth, History, Tradition, and Modernity in Indian English drama, which is entirely native in content and form, and derives its sustenance from Sanskrit drama, which is considered to be divine in origin involving Brahma who entrusted this task to Bharata Muni. And Bharata Muni's *Natyasastra* is a work of this kind. In India, drama flourishes today in regional languages, like Marathi, Bengali, Tamil, and Kannada. But Indian English drama suffers from certain drawbacks. It lacks the Indian ethos; it could not solve the conflict between the inner and outer worlds (as discovered in the plays of Rabindranath Tagore and Sri Aurobindo); and it is unsuitable to perform on the stage. In this connection, Prof. K.R. Srinivasa Iyengar rightly remarks, "Modern Indian dramatic writing in English is neither rich in quantity, nor, on the whole, of high quality" (1984: 226). The post-Independence scenario is, however, a bit heartening. The plays of Girish Karnad, Badal Sircar, Vijay Tendulkar, and Asif Currimbhoy show a skilled control of the tool, of language, and of dialogue. Indian English drama should use much and more of Indian Myth, History, and Culture to render it more readable and arresting.

The ninth essay/paper concentrates on contemporary Indian English Poetry and studies it from the viewpoint of culture and identity. Prof. K.R. Srinivasa Iyengar uses the term 'new' in place of 'contemporary' to describe 'modern' or 'modernist' poetry. Among the poets of older generation, three names are outstanding, though they cannot be called 'contemporary'. They are Toru Dutt (1856-1877), Rabindranath Tagore (1861-1941), and Sri Aurobindo (1872-1950). From the cultural viewpoint, I have briefly studied such 'new' poets as Nissim Ezekiel, P. Lal (who stand at the threshold of 'contemporaneity'), Dom Moraes, A.K. Ramanujan, Keki N. Daruwalla, Kamala Das, Jayanta Mahapatra, Shiv K. Kumar, R. Parthasarathy, and a few others. I have also studied some women poets, like Eunice de Souza, Sujata Bhatt, Meena Alexander, and Smita Agrawal. At the end of this paper, I express my optimistic view about the growth and enrichment of Indian English Poetry.

The tenth essay/paper maintains that culture and literature are the two areas which have undergone drastic changes in the recent past. For a consideration of culture, two texts—*The Wretched of the Earth* (1961) by Frantz Fanon and *The Location of Culture* (1994) by Homi K. Bhabha—have been specially studied. It has been suggested that 'culture' has now become 'pluculture' or 'multiculture', and that it has crossed the national boundaries and assumed global character. As for literature, it may be seen as a cultural construct along with education. In his book, *Literary Theory: A Very Short Introduction* (1997 and 2000: 43), Jonathan Culler is of the same view. Modernism begins in English literature after the First World War (1914-1918). Postmodernism is usually regarded as a continuation of 'the counter traditional experiments of modernism', and also as a departure from 'the modernist elitist forms of expression' by resorting to the models of 'mass culture' (as discovered in film, television, newspaper cartoons, and popular music). The theory of Colonialism/Postcolonialism is evidently linked to historical and political events. Edward Said's *Orientalism* (1978), Bill Ashcroft, Gareth Griffiths, and Helen Tiffin's *The Empire Writes Back* (1989), and Homi Bhabha's *The Location of Culture* (1994) are some of the seminal works in this area of criticism. The present paper also takes into account the concept of Feminism and the theory of Deconstruction in brief.

The eleventh essay/paper takes up Nation, Culture, and Identity for consideration. A nation is usually defined as "a large number of people of mainly common descent, language, history, etc., usually inhabiting a territory bounded by defined limits and forming a society under one government" (C.O.D., 6th ed. 1975: 725). The views of Benedict Anderson, Joseph Stalin, and Bipin Chandra Pal are taken into account here. Anderson considers nation as an 'imagined community' created by 'a radically secular and modern imagination', but it is not imaginary or fictitious. Stalin thinks that a nation is "primarily a community, a definite community of people" (*Works*, II, 1954: 300-381). And Bipin Chandra Pal, a famous nationalist leader of India, opines that "...territorial unity is an essential condition of nationality, but not of raciality" (1916 and 2002: 3). Pal thinks that a nation must have territorial unity or geographical unity. Culture is defined as "the beliefs, way of life, art, and customs that are shared and accepted by people in a particular society" (*Longman Dictionary of Contemporary English,* 1978 and 2003: 382). It is often linked to national culture. It becomes transnational culture—multinational or plucultural—when it crosses the national boundaries. Homi K. Bhabha calls it the culture of 'global cosmopolitanism' (1994 and 2007: xiv). Within India itself, there is a vast cultural diversity, as noticed by Pt. Jawaharlal Nehru in his insightful work, *The Discovery of India* (1946). Nehru pleads for 'unity in diversity'. As for Identity, it is akin to a sense of 'belonging'. Identity is recognition and is deeply connected to national identity and cultural identity. Besides the critical theories relating to Nation, Culture, and Identity, this paper examines Rushdie's *Midnight's Children* (1981) and *The Enchantress of Florence* (2008), Arundhati Roy's *The God of Small Things* (1997), Jhumpa Lahiri's *The Lowland* (2013), Neel Mukherjee's *The Lives of Others* (2014), Aravind Adiga's

The White Tiger (2008), Jeet Thayil's *Narcopolis* (2012), and Jerry Pinto's *Em and the Big Hoom* (2012) as samples of one or the other critical theory.

The twelfth essay/paper, the last one in this anthology, studies Globalization as a tool of the expansion of capitalist economy or industry crossing the boundaries of the nation-state, the local, the individual society, history, and culture. In fact, the local and the national are getting transformed today under the impact of Globalization. The theory of Nation and Culture is also undergoing a drastic change because of Globalization. Homi K. Bhabha calls it 'global cosmopolitanism' (as mentioned earlier). Clearly, the forces of Globalization have given immense boost to the capitalist entrepreneurship and the consumerist (or materialist) culture. Fredric Jameson in his book, *The Cultures of Globalization* (1998 and 2004) written in collaboration with Masao Miyoshi, maintains the view that "globalization is a communicational concept, which alternately masks and transmits cultural or economic meanings"(55). In the final analysis, Globalization is helpful in promoting mass-production and mall-culture, also in creating employment opportunities, but it has to be controlled by considerations of the overall safety and welfare of mankind.

The essays/papers put together in this compilation offer more or less a clear picture of the theory and practice of contemporary English criticism. The compilation covers up the significant literary theories of the 20th and 21st centuries, and excludes those of the Greek masters (Plato, Aristotle, Longinus, etc.) and those of previous English critics (Sidney, Dryden, Pope, Arnold, etc.). The contributions of the Great English Romantics (Wordsworth, Coleridge, Shelley, and Keats) have been briefly studied in the fourth essay/paper here in relation to the critical formulations of T.S. Eliot. I know, the compilation is selective and limited in scope, and there is a possibility of its further expansion. I appeal to the readers of this critical anthology to judge it in the light of its selective scope and elective approach.

Amar Nath Dwivedi

Contents

Preface .... *iv*

1. Voice of the Voiceless: Subaltern Writings in English 1
2. Diasporic Writings in English 14
3. New English Literatures of the Colonized 26
4. T.S. Eliot's Criticism and the Great English Romantics: A Comparative View 41
5. Native Modernity in Indian English Fiction 52
6. Postmodernism in Indian English Fiction: Issues and Challenges 62
7. Magic Realism in Rushdie's *The Enchantress of Florence* 79
8. Myth, History, Tradition and Modernity in Indian English Drama 86
9. Contemporary Indian English Poetry: A Study in Culture and Identity 96
10. Changing Paradigms of Culture and Literature 112

11. Nation, Culture and Identity: Theory and Texts in the 21st Century 122

12. Reading Globalization 134

Suggestions for Further Reading 143

Index 146

1

Voice of the Voiceless: Subaltern Writings in English

At the very outset, we must understand that this essay/paper is going to discuss in some detail the writings in English of those authors who have raised their voice for the voiceless; for the suppressed and oppressed classes; for the lower sections of society. In other words, the essay/paper will concentrate on "recovering the histories and perspectives of marginalised people—be they women, non-Whites, non-Europeans, the lower classes and oppressed castes...."[1] These people have suffered immensely in the days of colonialism and even postcolonialism, and in the Indian context they comprise the scheduled castes and the scheduled tribes, the lower classes like *Dalits*, sweepers and scavengers, *Chandals,* and women. We will examine here how writers have responded or reacted to the living conditions of these people in their creative works.

Gayatri Chakravorty Spivak, in her insightful essay, "Can the Subaltern Speak?" (1985), powerfully raises the issue of the 'subaltern' or oppressed subject. She defines the 'subaltern' as "a person without lines of social mobility."[2] She suggests that it is impossible to recover the voice of the 'subaltern' in a stultifying society. In the initial stage of her essay, Spivak is concerned with Marx's concept of class struggle between the haves and the have-nots, between the power-wielding class and the working class. She mentions that Marx's concept of a class is "artificial and economic", and the economic agency or *interest* is impersonal because it is "systemic and heterogeneous."[3] She dwells on Marx possibly to point out that he does not consider women as a class demanding social justice. Then Spivak speaks of a radical critic like Foucault who believes that oppressed subjects can speak for themselves, as he can't visualize the repressive power of colonialism and its intersection with the paralyzing hold of patriarchy in the social context. Spivak talks of Foucault's locating "one case of epistemic violence...in the redefinition of madness at the end of the European eighteenth century"[4] in the light of what Napoleon Bonaparte had done. While talking of the epistemic violence, Spivak takes up the colonial debate on widow immolation in India to illustrate her viewpoint. The woman, whose husband was no more, was forced to burn on her husband's pyre willy-nilly and considering *sati* as an evil social practice, Raja Rammohan Roy fought against it. Spivak maintains that "the ideological construction of gender keeps the male dominant" and that "the subaltern has no history and cannot speak, the subaltern as female is even more deeply in shadow."[5] The history of female repression can be read in a sentence like "White men are saving brown women from brown men." This possessive colonial attitude of Afro-Americans towards the Blacks gets transformed into an imposed, so-called 'self-willed' immolation for widows in India. Tyrannical repression of women holds the centre-stage in any consideration of the 'subaltern' question.

Benita Parry, a well-known postcolonial critic, points out that Spivak's argument about "doubly-oppressed native women" serves to "constrain the development of an anti-imperialist critique."[6] This kind of critique has also been advocated by Edward Said in his *Orientalism* (1978) and Homi K. Bhabha in his *The Location of Culture* (1994). Parry suggests that Spivak's insistence on the voicelessness of the non-elite or subaltern woman is not judiciously conceived. She says, "It will be argued that the lacunae in Spivak's learned disquisitions issue from a theory assigning an absolute power to the hegemonic discourse in constituting and disarticulating the native."[7] Very clearly, the theory referred to here is related to Spivak's attempts at "theorizing the silence of the doubly-oppressed subaltern woman" (first by the White colonists and then by the patriarchal system), and her theorem on imperialism's epistemic violence "extends to posting the native, male and female, as a historically-muted subject."[8] Even within the confines of this discourse, a scholar like Lata Mani *does* find evidence of woman's voice, and Mani's dissent is well noted by Spivak.[9] Another scholar, Chandra Talpade Mohanty, who is presently based in Ithaca, New York, seems to side with Lata Mani when she argues that discourses of representation, as formulated by western feminist writers on 'Third World Women', should not be confused with material realities, and that it is possible to locate traces of woman's voice there where she comes out as a healer, an ascetic, a singer of sacred songs, an artisan and artist. Mohanty pleads for feminist solidarity through anti-capitalist struggles.[10]

The above-noted critics and their valued opinions clearly bring out their divergent attitudes towards womankind. Hereafter we will consider the treatment of womankind by some well-known female creative writers like Nayantara Sahgal, Shashi Deshpande, Githa Hariharan, Arundhati Roy, and Manju Kapur in Indian English writing. Some others like Kamala Markandaya and Kamala Das among Indian writers, Bharati Mukherji among diasporic writers, and Toni Morrison among Afro-American writers may be briefly examined here to ascertain their views on this vital issue. For one thing, male writers are left out of this consideration in order to present only the first-hand experiences of womankind.

Kamala Markandaya and Nayantara Sahgal, the two novelists of the older generation, and Kamala Das, an eminent poet of yester years, have diversely dealt with women and their grappling issues. Markandaya, for whom I have vigorously pleaded that she should be raised to the position of "the Big Three"[11] and made one of "the Four Wheels" of the Indian English Fiction[12], sharply focuses on female characters struggling hard for their survival; for example, Rukmani in *Nectar in a Sieve* (1954). Other women characters in Markandaya's novels, such as Mira in *Some Inner Fury* (1955), Sarojini in *A Silence of Desire* (1960), Caroline in *Possession* (1963), Vasantha in *The Nowhere Man* (1972), and the two contrasted sisters, Lalitha and Saroja, in *Two Virgins* (1973), are also seen struggling in their lives for other reasons—for love or passion, for being childless, for possessive instincts, for cultural divide and racial hatred, for attraction towards the glamour of the city or repulsion from it. What I intend to suggest here is that the female characters of Markandaya are sometimes muted (like Rukmani and Sarojini) and sometimes vocal (the remaining ones mentioned above); sometimes they suffer silently, while at others they raise their voice.

From the feminist point of view, Nayantara Sahgal is a significant name to recall. Her novels beginning with *Prison and Chocolate Cake* (1954), through *The Day in Shadow* (1971), to *Rich Like Us* (1983), and *Mistaken Identity* (1988), are largely concerned with some raging socio-political issues as well as with 'the Woman Question'. As regards 'the Woman Question', we can take up the example of *The Day in Shadow* wherein the theme of the woman as-a-victim surfaces in the story of Simrit, who is married to Som, a domineering husband indeed. Simrit does not have the freedom to choose even in domestic matters, such as 'chair covers and curtains'. It is ultimately Som's wishes and choices that prevail, and this creates a smothering effect upon her. When Som decides to have no more children, she feels the stranglehold of their sexual and marital relationship because it is a one-sided decision. Now she feels complete marginalization from Som's world and slowly yet steadily drifts towards another man called Raj for her emotional fulfilment. But the boyfriend later marries another woman, leaving Simrit to her grudge and grouse and eventually sinking into silence. As an educated woman and a professional writer, she now develops greater involvement with nature, not with men and their manners. The great feminist thinker, Simone de Beauvoir, thinks that "nature represents what woman herself represents for man, herself and her negation, a kingdom and a place of exile; the whole in the guise of the other."[13] Sexual exploitation and survival, adultery and extra-marital relationships are witnessed in Sahgal's other novels—for example, Kusum in *A Time to be Happy* (1958), Rashmi in *The Time of Morning* (1965), Saroj in *Storm in Chandigarh* (1969), etc.

Kamala Das is generally known as the poet of love and sex. Although some scholars have tried to trace purity in her love by putting her in the Mirabai-Lord Krishna tradition, they are not correct in doing so. Poem after poem she speaks of "a hunger/ to take in with greed, like a forest-fire that/ Consumes..." ("Forest Fire", *Summer in Calcutta*, 1965, p. 51), "the womb's blinded hunger, the muted whisper/ at the core" ("Captive", *The Descendants,* p. 17), "That was the only kind of love,/ This hacking at each other's parts/ Like convicts hacking, breaking clods/ At noon" ("Convicts", *The Descendants*, p. 26), and "Cowering/ Beneath your monstrous ego I ate the magic loaf and/ Became a dwarf. I lost my will and reason..." ("The Old Playhouse", *The Old Playhouse & Other Poems*, 1973, p. 1). Kamala Das in her life was a dispirited wife and repeatedly complained against her husband. In one of her articles, she writes:

> My husband was immersed in his office-work, and after work there was the dinner, followed by sex. Where was there any time left for him to see the sea or the dark buffaloes of the slopes?[14]

To get rid of this situation of boredom, despair and strangulation, Mrs. Das seeks solace in another man's arms. A clear-cut hint at the fact is to be had in her poem "The Looking Glass", wherein she says:

> Getting a man to love you is easy
> Only be honest about your wants as
> Woman. Stand nude before the glass with him
> So that he sees himself the stronger one
> And believes it so, and you so much more
> Softer, younger, lovelier....

and again:

> Gift him all,
> Give him what makes you woman, the scent of
> Long hair, the musk of sweat between the breasts,
> The warm shock of menstrual blood, and all your
> Endless female hungers.
>
> (*The Descendants*, p. 25)

If such passages bring out the painful cry of a helpless woman, they also hint at the emotional cravings and the freedom to enjoy their fulfilment at the legitimate or illegitimate source. Kamala Das, in such passages, becomes the champion of woman's cause, like Preeta Bhargava pleading for female freedom in sexual relations in the 1913 Literary Fest held at Jaipur recently.

Perhaps no one has better expressed the silence or speechlessness of womankind than Shashi Deshpande in her novels. Saru or Sarita, the protagonist of *The Dark Holds No Terrors* (1980), become a doctor of fame and a better earning member of the family, and this breeds a sense of inferiority in her husband of meagre means who turns a sadist in his nocturnal meetings with her. So, in her utter helplessness, she goes away to her Baba who advises her to be with Manu, her husband. Where is the solution to her personal problems? A similar situation obtains in *That Long Silence* (1988), where Jaya and Mohan develop an estranged relationship, so much so that they are not even on talking terms. At last, it is Jaya who decides to break the ice of silence. Thus, Deshpande treads the middle path as a feminist (if she is one at all), not the aggressive path of the Western feminists. This is what prompts Mukta Atrey and Viney Kirpal to remark in their perceptive study on Shashi Deshpande as follows: "So what makes Indian women 'feminists' different is the fact that they raise their voice against social injustice and oppression of woman rather than ask for her freedom from the institution of marriage and family."[15]

Another woman writer of repute is Githa Hariharan who has also tackled 'the Woman Question' with intelligence and understanding. Her two novels—*The Thousand Faces of Night* (1992) and *When Dreams Travel* (1999)—bring out some memorable women characters. Devi, an America-educated girl, in the first novel returns to India and accepts an arranged marriage on the insistence of her mother Sita, a self-respecting lady of sacrificing nature, but Devi is not happy with her husband who stays at home for only ten days in a month and then goes out, to Bangalore, to serve a multinational toothpaste company. Her barrenness increases her tension and irritation. In a huff, she leaves for Delhi to join her romantic lover Gopal, a singer by profession. Getting disillusioned with him, she returns to her mother, not to her husband. Hariharan's second novel, *When Dreams Travel*, depicts two powerful women characters, Shahrzad and Duniyazad, who make use of their talent and also body to tame a repressible king called Shahryar. Of the two women, Duniyazad becomes a liberated woman by establishing physical relations with her elder sister's husband.

Arundhati Roy also portrays such a woman in an arresting manner in her novel, *The God of Small Things* (1997), and this woman called Ammukutty is a divorcee with two children. She belongs to an upper stratum of Syrian Christians and dreams of a youngman named Velutha of a lower class. She is a great daydreamer[16] and crosses all bounds of societal norms when she starts meeting the youngman in a haunted house across the river Meenachal. Baby Kochamma lodges a report with the police that Velutha, a parvan (an untouchable), has forced himself upon Ammu, and on the basis of this report Velutha is arrested, beaten with boots and batons, and thrown into the lock-up where he dies in midnight. The incident gives great shock to Ammu who also breathes her last subsequently. At that time, she is simply "thirty-one. Not old, not young, but a viable-die-able age" (*The God of Small Things*, p. 161). Thus, the tyrannical traditional society has taken away the lives of two loving souls. Ammu is, no doubt, a liberated woman or 'feminist' asserting her rights over her body, as Simone de Beauvoir would put it,[17] but the eventual outcome is tragic and disastrous.

If Arundhati Roy is the novelist of the twentieth century, Manju Kapur is one of the twenty-first century. Manju Kapur, a Lady Lecturer at Miranda College in Delhi, has published five novels[18] to this day, and in her novels, she has largely dwelt on women's exploitation and sufferings. Virmati in her first novel *Difficult Daughters* (1998), for instance, enters into a love marriage with a Professor of Amritsar, who refuses to leave his first wife. Consequently, she ends up being marginalised by her own family and despised by her husband. Her story is told by her only daughter Ida against the background of the Independence movement of the 1940s and the subsequent trauma of Partition. Virmati wilts under the hostile gaze of Ganga, her husband's first wife, with whom she has to live. She loses all sense of identity. The repeated clandestine visits of the fatal Professor cause the loss of her employers' confidence in her at Nahan (H.P.) and she loses her employment there. Thus, Virmati's tale is a tale of sufferings, exploitation and repression. Even the fate of Astha and Peepli Trivedi in *A Married Woman* (2003), Sona and Nisha in *Home* (2006), Nina in *Immigrant* (2008), and Shagun and Ishita in *Custody* (2011) does not hold a bright prospect for them. Out of sheer desperation, some of these women even resort to lesbianism.

No one has better represented the diasporic situation of an Indian immigrant, especially a woman, than perhaps Bharati Mukherjee (born 1940), now a naturalized American citizen (since 1988). In her novels like *Wife* (1975) and *Jasmine* (1989), she focuses on the experience of a woman who is forced to face her marginalization with her own culture and also within a foreign culture, both of which are impinged in patriarchal ideology. The quest for identity is the primary concern of her female protagonists who are inescapably caught in the flux of tradition and modernity. Dimple Dasgupta, for example, in Mukherjee's novel *Wife* accepts an arranged marriage with Amit Basu, an engineer who is due to immigrate to Canada and the U.S.A. in the near future. On the objections of her mother-in-law, Mrs. Basu, Dimple's name is changed to Nandini, and this change is an impingement upon her individuality. Soon she becomes pregnant, but she does not like her pregnancy and induces miscarriage by skipping rope until her legs are numb. Reaching America, she expects a changed life, may be an employment as a librarian, may be a freedom from cramping marital status. She meets Ina Mullick, a liberated housewife who is "more American than Americans,"[19] and who dazzles her with her air of sophistication, her command of English, and her 'Women Lib' advice to "crack the whip".[20] Dimple, being confined to home and hearth, starts watching T.V. shows too frequently, and this fact distances her from Amit. T.V. programmes are least demanding, whereas Amit is ever demanding and commanding. She drifts much and more towards freedom-loving Milt Glasser, and in a fit of depression and frustration she murders Amit. Commenting on Dimple, Brinda Bose writes thus:

> Dimple has become a prisoner of the ghetto and being an educated and thinking woman she is unable to accept

> the contradictions of this existence; hence her descent into depression, madness and murder.[21]

Her mad action reminds us of Maya's pushing Gautama down the terrace in Anita Desai's *Cry, the Peacock* (1963).

Among the Afro-American writers, Toni Morrison stands out as a representative voice of the Blacks. In her novels she highlights the predicament and hardships of Black women in a graphic way. If *The Bluest Eye* (1970) is a recordation of the defiling of a black girl, named Pecola, by her own father Chally Breedlove in the presence of her helpless mother Pauline, then *Sula* (1973) narrates the bonds of love between two girlfriends, Sula and Nel, and their subsequent estrangement after Sula establishes sexual relationship with Nel's husband. Sula is regarded as the very embodiment of evil who passively watches her mother burn to death. The cruelty of mother-figure comes out vividly in Morrison's fifth novel, *Beloved* (1987), which earned for her the 1988 Pulitzer Prize for Fiction. The mother, Sethe Suggs, kills her infant daughter rather than allowing her to grow and get enslaved. Her other novels—*Jazz* (1992), *Paradise* (1999), *Love* (2003), and *A Mercy* (2008)—also portray the various shades of mothering and motherhood. For example, *A Mercy*, her latest novel, brings to light the horrors of the system of slavery where a helpless slave mother offers her pre-teen daughter Florens to a buyer called Jacob Vaark, an Anglo-Dutch trader, hoping that she will find a better home. The serious thought that Morrison gives to the concerns of mothers shackled in slavery recalls to our minds, by way of contrast, Buchi Emecheta, a well-known woman writer of Nigeria who exults in delineating the blisses of motherhood in her novel, *The Joys of Motherhood* (New York: George Braziller, 1979).

After having dealt with the different facets of womanhood as depicted by the aforementioned creative writers, now we turn our attention to the treatment of the lower classes of people by writers like Munshi Premchand in *Godan* (1957 English ed.), Mulk Raj Anand in *Untouchable* (1935), and Arundhati Roy in *The God of Small Things* (1997). *Godan* is a story of stark realism and portrays the tragedy and pathos in the hard lives of Hori Ram and his wife Dhania. They are a poor couple, hardworking and honest, and have desired all along to have a cow of their own to feed their son Gobar with plenty of milk. Exploited by the Zamindar, Hori has to work hard in the fields and return home late in the evening. But till the very end, he could not manage a cow. Hori catches the loo while working in the fields and sinks quickly. His wife has no money to buy a cow and offer her in charity to Datadeen, the village brahmin. Dhania's last words are quotable her: "Maharaj, there's neither a cow, nor a calf nor any money in the house. This is all the money [twenty annas] I have; this is all I can give. Take this in place of the cow."[22] Saying so, she collapses on the ground. The backbone-breaking poverty of the peasants of India under the feudal system is marvellously revealed in *Godan*, which remains "unparalleled and unsurpassed in the whole fiction of India."[23]

Mulk Raj Anand's *Untouchable*, as the title clearly indicates, is directly based on the miserable conditions of the sweepers and scavengers doing round and cleaning latrines. The central character, Bakha, is a young man of fourteen who experiences alienation and segregation in the Hindu society. He is a sensitive young man who wants changes in life. The novelist records the event happening in a day of his life. Initially, he is an admirer of the Whiteman and puts on dresses like a Sahib, as he is angry with the hypocrisy and pretensions of the Hindus. He is humiliated by a caste Hindu on the pretext of touching him inadvertently; the crowd also boos and jeers him. His sister, Sohini, is insulted by the temple-priest, Pt. Kali Nath, but his timely arrival saves her honour. Sohini is a beautiful girl whose problems arise from her caste as well as her sex. Her attractive figure awakens jealously in Gulabo, the washerwoman. Later in the day, Bakha carries a wounded child home, but the child's mother, instead of commending him, finds fault with him for having polluted her child. Thereafter, Bakha attends a meeting addressed by Gandhiji and is filled with a sense of self-respect when Gandhi remarks that the untouchables (harijans) are 'cleaners of Hindu society'. Thus Bakha's evolution from a blind imitation of the colonizer to a realisation of the need for self-assertion signifies "a shift from dependence to autonomy and the release of the subaltern from the position of liminality."[24] Like Bakha in *Untouchable*, we have Munoo (a poor lad being exploited by Mrs. Mainwaring) in *Coolie* (1936) and Bhikhu (the son of Laxmi, an untouchable woman) in *The Road* (1961) are described as "inscriptions of the colonized subaltern in the discourse of fiction...."[25]

A consideration of the subaltern studies will be possibly incomplete without a reference to *The God of Small Things* (1997). In this novel, as noted earlier, Arundhati Roy exposes the miserable conditions of the paravans (untouchables) through the ages. The owners of the Ayemen house, Pappachi and Mammachi, would not allow the paravans into their house: "They were not allowed to touch anything that 'Touchables' touched. Caste Hindus and Caste Christians."[26] They were not allowed to walk on public roads, not allowed to cover their upper bodies, not allowed to carry umbrellas. These social restrictions were faithfully followed by Kelan (Velutha's grandfather) and his son, but they were flagrantly flouted by Velutha. And the result was his tragic, untimely death in the police custody, leaving behind "no footprints in sand, no ripples in water, no image in mirrors."[27]

To conclude, I have tried to highlight, in the foregoing pages, miserable conditions of the subaltern as discovered in the creative works of a few outstanding writers. The subaltern includes women, untouchables, and people of lower castes and classes. Their voice might have remained muted and marginalized in earlier times, but now they have become conscious of their rights and privileges and are raising their resonant voice in every sphere of human activity—social, political, religious, and literary. They have now definitely moved from Erasure to Assertion.[28] In this way, the voice of the voiceless is now audible on almost every platform of literary discussions.

Notes

1. Ania Loomba, *Colonialism/Postcolonialism* (1998; London & New York: Routledge, 2001 rpt.), p. 231.
2. Gayatri Chakravorty Spivak, "Can the Subaltern Speak?" *The Postcolonial Studies Reader* (1995), eds. Bill Ashcroft, Gareth Griffiths & Helen Tiffin (Oxford & New York: Routledge, 2nd ed. 2006), pp. 28-37. This quotation is found on p. 28.
3. *Ibid*., p. 29.

4. *Ibid.*, p. 31.
5. *Ibid.*, p. 32.
6. Benita Parry, "Problems in Current Theories of Colonial Discourse," *The Post-colonial Studies Reader*, eds. Ashcroft, Griffiths & Tiffin (2nd ed., 2006), p. 44.
7. *Idem.*
8. *Ibid.*, p. 45.
9. See "Note 8" at the close of "Can the Subaltern Speak?", *The Post-colonial Studies Reader* (2006), p. 36.
10. Chandra Talpade Mohanty, "Feminist Solidarity Through Anticapitalist Struggles", *The Post-colonial Studies Reader* (2006), pp. 485-89.

    As a material realist, Mohanty records: "Clearly there is the ubiquitous global teenage girl factory worker, the domestic worker, and the sex worker. There is also the migrant/immigrant service worker, the refugee, the victim of war crimes, the woman-of-color prisoner who happens to be a mother and drug user, the consumer-housewife, and so on. There is also the mother-of-the-nation/religious bearer of traditional culture and morality." (pp. 486-87).
11. In his article "The Big Three" appearing in *Indian Writing in English,* ed. Ramesh Mohan (Madras: Orient Longman Ltd., 1978), pp. 26-36, William Walsh mentions Mulk Raj Anand, R.K. Narayan and Raja Rao as the three great novelists.
12. A.N. Dwivedi, ed. *Studies in Contemporary Indian Fiction in English* (Allahabad: Kitab Mahal, 1987), p. 10.
13. Simone de Beauvoir, *The Second Sex*, tr. H.M. Parshley (1949; New York: Alfred A. Knopf, 1993), pp. 710-11.
14. Kamala Das, "I Have Lived Beautifully," *Debonir,* III, No. 5 (15 May 1975), p. 41.
15. Mukta Atrey and Viney Kirpal, "Introduction", *Shashi Deshpande: A Feminist Study of Her Fiction* (Delhi: B.R. Publishing Corporation, 1998), pp. 5-6.
16. Ammu dreams of 'one-armed man' day in and day out. Who is this man? The novelist suggests that he is—

    The God of Loss.
    The God of Small Things.
    The God of Goose Bumps and Sudden Smiles.

    —*The God of Small Things* (New Delhi: IndiaInk Publishing Co. Pvt. Ltd., 1997), p. 330.

17. Simone de Beauvoir suggests that 'feminism' envisions "economic independence and liberation from orthodox tradition of society", *The Second Sex*, ed. H.M. Parshley, p. 126.
18. Manju Kapur's five novels are *Difficult Daughters* (London: Faber & Faber, 1998), *A Married Woman* (London: Faber & Faber, 2003), *Home* (New Delhi: Random House, 2006), *Immigrant* (New Delhi: Random House, 2008), and *Custody* (New Delhi: Random House, 2011).
19. Bharati Mukherjee, *Wife* (New York: Fawcett Crest, 1975), p. 68.
20. *Ibid.,* p. 76.
21. Brinda Bose, "In Good Faith? Shadows of Hinduism on Expatriate Identity in the Fiction of Bharati Mukherjee," *And the Birds Began to Sing: Religion and Literature in Post-colonial Culture* (Amsterdam & New York: Rodopi, 1994), p. 293.
22. Premchand, *Godan*, trs. Jai Ratan and P. Lal (Mumbai: Jaico Publishing House, 1957, 25th impr. 2011), p. 339.
23. Cited from the inner cover of *Godan.*
24. C. Vijayasree, *Mulk Raj Anand: The Raj and the Writer* (Delhi: B.R. Publishing Corporation, 1998), p. 29.
25. *Ibid.*, p. 24.
26. Arundhati Roy, *The God of Small Things* (1997), pp. 73-74.
27. *Ibid.*, p. 216.
28. Alok Mukherjee, "Reading Sharankumar Limbale's *Towards an Aesthetic of Dalit Literature*: From Erasure to Assertion," *Towards an Aesthetic of Dalit Literature* (Hyderabad: Orient Blackswan Pvt. Ltd., 2010), pp. 1-18.

2
Diasporic Writings in English

The term 'diaspora' (Greek in origin, derived from 'diaspeiro') literally means a scattering or dispersion of a group of people to an alien land, away from their traditional homelands. In olden days, the term was used for the worldwide scattering of the Jews outside Palestine. Nowadays, it is applied to "a number of ethnic and racial groups"[1] living abroad. So, the term has a history behind it and also a topical relevance.

We are mainly concerned, at the moment, with the writings of the Indian diaspora in English. Such writings are also known as 'expatriate writings' or 'immigrant writings'. The diasporic writings are generally marked by a sense of isolation and far-removedness from the mother-country. Hence such words as immigrant, exile and refugee are also applied to this brand of writing. 'Immigrant' indicates a location, a foreign settlement, and a physical movement, while 'exile' evokes "a variety of relationships with the mother-country—alienation, forced exile, self-imposed exile, political exile and so on."[2] The word 'refugee' denotes a person taking refuge in a foreign land for safety or for self-fulfilment. The diasporic writings combine all these features and attitudes in their texture.

The aesthetic of 'Diaspora' emanates from the colonial experience of the people of the subject-nation who, for want of opportunities of employment at home or due to exploitation by the colonizer, shift to another country. The immigrants, not necessarily indentured labourers, exercise a great impact on the culture, society and history of that country. At the same time, they nostalgically recall their motherland—its custom, culture, language and people—and creatively use these things in their writings if they are gifted intellectuals.

The main theorists of Diaspora are Edward Said, Gayatri Chakravorty Spivak and Homi Bhabha. These theorists are also the exponents of 'Colonialism' and 'Postcolonialism'. But while 'Colonialism and Postcolonialism' refer to the political and historical aspects of a country, the Diasporic theory is more preoccupied with the question of centrality, hybridity, ambience, transculturation of the people. Diasporic writing is concerned with what Edward Said calls "not only of a basic geographical distinction but also a whole sense of 'interests'."[3] Edward Said's *Orientalism* (1978) envisages the Orient as 'the Other' that is dominated by the Occident in the power-game. This naturally allots 'an inferior status' to the 'subject-races', and the sense of inferiority, insecurity, joblessness, or the dream of a better prospect outside is the cause of the dispersion of the Diaspora. Edward Said's theory that "knowledge gives power, more power requires more knowledge, and so on in an increasingly profitable dialectic of information and control"[4] corroborates this idea. Gayatri Chakravorty Spivak, who convincingly evolves the notion of 'subalternity', also believes that 'the third World' (Said's 'the other World') is a creation of the West which distorts, even resorts to violence towards the non-Western cultures. Spivak's theory of 'subalternity' (i.e., being of lower status) encompasses women, Blacks, the colonized and the working class. Her famous essay "Can the Subaltern Speak?"[5] mainly addresses itself to the 'muteness' of women in postcolonial societies. In contrast to Said's emphatic assertion of 'identity' or 'centrality' that an exile or expatriate should seek in order to save himself/herself, Homi Bhabha upholds the tenet of 'hybridity' in the cultural context, and his poetics of 'disjunctive temporality', which is analogous to Salman Rushdie's notion of 'broken mirror' about the immigrant, makes a 'mimicry' of the notion of 'centrality'. Bhabha's temporality "creates a signifying time for the inscription of cultural incommensurability."[6]

The Diasporic writers are now scattered throughout the world, and are found in such diverse places as Fiji, Trinidad, and Guyana (where they are in minority), and in Malaysia, Mauritius and East Africa, and in western countries like Britain, America, Canada and Australia (where they are in good numbers).

Right from the dawn of Indian Writing in English, the talented Indians have been going abroad and reaping a rich literary harvest out of a commingling of cultures and languages. Prof. K.R. Srinivasa Iyengar in his book, *Indian Writing in English* (1962), thinks that "modern Indian literature" begins with Raja Rammohun Roy (1774-1833), who "was destined to act as a bridge between India and England,"[7] and we know that Roy was a master of English prose. The Dutts and the Ghoses frequently shuttled between Europe and India. Who does not know the life-history of Michael Madhusudan Dutt, Toru Dutt, Romesh Chunder Dutt, Manmohan Ghose, and Sri Aurobindo? They all were born Indians but shifted to the West for academic and literary pursuits. In due course, they produced works of lasting value. Madhusudan's *Meghnad Badha* (which was rendered in English in 1879), Toru's *Ancient Ballads* (1882) and her earlier book of translations *A Sheaf Gleaned in French Fields* (1876), Romesh Chunder's skilled translations of *Sansar* (*The Lake of Palms*) (1902) and *Madhavi Kankan* (*The Slave Girl of Agra*) (1909), Manmohan's *Love Songs and Elegies* (1898) and Sri Aurobindo's *Savitri* (1950-51) are some of the outstanding works by all means. The award of the Nobel Prize in literature to Thakur Rabindranath Tagore for his *Gitanjali* in 1913 stimulated a number of authors to write in English. Sarojini Naidu, M.K. Gandhi, Jawaharlal Nehru, Mulk Raj Anand, R.K. Narayan, Raja Rao and a host of other authors expressed themselves in English with ease and command. But all these authors returned to India after their short or a little longer stay in the West.

The diasporic writing proper has, however, a worldwide context, and it includes writers of both old and new generations who have left India and settled abroad. Of the old generation of such writers, we may mention Kamala Markandaya, B. Rajan, Santha Rama Rau, Bharati Mukherjee, Anita Desai, Salman Rushdie, Vikram Seth, V.S. Naipaul, Nirad Chaudhari, Amitav Ghosh, Ved Mehta and A.K. Ramanujan. The younger generation of writers includes Kiran Desai, Saros Cowasjee, Cyril Dabydeen, Tilottama Rajan, Uma Parmeswaran, Ashish Gupta, Rohinton

Mistry, Neil Bissoondath, M.G. Vassanji, Pico Iyer, Gita Mehta, Chitra Banerjee Divakaruni, Meena Alexander, Jhumpa Lahiri, Sujata Bhatt, and Mena Abdullah.

Kamala Markandaya, who was married to Mr. Taylor and who might be called "the Fourth Wheel"[8] of Indian English Novel, has been a prolific writer, with ten novels to her credit. Many of her novels deal with the theme of East-West encounter, and in them the characters are drawn from both India and England. We come across in them 'nostalgic longings for India'—one of the salient features of the diasporic writing. Markandaya's novels—*Some Inner Fury* (1955), *Possession* (1963), *The Coffer Dams* (1969), *The Nowhere Man* (1972), *The Golden Honeycomb* (1977), and *Pleasure City* (1982) are to be marked in this connection.

B. Rajan, who is more known as a literary critic of Milton, Yeats and Eliot, than as a creative writer, has published two novels, *The Dark Dancer* (1958) and *Too Long in the West* (1961). Like his protagonist Krishnan in *The Dark Dancer*, B. Rajan has lived too long in the West—in England, America and Canada. Finally, he settled in Toronto (Canada). Here his daughter, Tilottama Rajan, must be mentioned as an authoress of *Myth in a Metal Mirror* (1967), which is a poetical collection containing 36 poems in all, though she belongs to the younger generation of diasporic writers.

Santha Rama Rau (whose full name is Vasanthi Rama Rau Bowers) was educated in England and America and was married to an American. She eventually settled in America and has authored such books as *Home to India* (1945), *Remember the House* (1956), *Gifts of Passage* (1961), and *The Adventures* (1971). Very often she is not considered an Indian writer, reminding us of the case of Bharati Mukherjee, and yet Prof. S.K. Desai in his critical book, on this author, argues that Rau "has essentially an Indian identity."[9] Rau is well-known for her scripting of the dramatic version of E.M. Forster's *A Passage to India*.

Bharati Mukherjee comes close on the heels of Santha Rama Rau. Though she, like Markandaya, retains her maiden name, she is much more westernized or better Americanized. She has written a few novels like *The Tiger's Daughter* (1973), *Wife* (1975), *Darkness* (1985), and *Jasmine* (1990). She represents the Indian woman in a cross-cultural context. She is out to seek a new identity for herself, but it turns out to be a broken identity. The female protagonists of Mukherjee's novels usually suffer from a sense of frustration and loneliness (for example, Dimple Dasgupta in *Wife*). Mukherjee collaborated with her husband, Clark Blaise, in writing a novel, *Days and Nights in Calcutta* (1977), which is actually "an autobiographical summation of her [Mukherjee's] return to her country after fourteen years of absence in North America."[10]

Anita Desai had become a diasporic writer of eminence for some time. Back in New Delhi, she produced a number of novels mainly portraying the abnormal and hypersensitive women in untoward situations. Her novels like *Cry, The Peacock* (1963), *Voices in the City* (1965), *Bye-Bye Blackbird* (1971), and *Fire on the Mountain* (1977) are to be specially marked in this connection. One of Anita's frequently used subjects is the cross-cultural contact between the East and the West and the resultant sense of alienation and frustration in her dominant characters.

It must be mentioned here that her daughter, Kiran Desai (born 1971) is also a diasporic writer now living in America and has produced two novels to her credit, *Hullabaloo Under the Guava Orchard* (1999) and *The Inheritance of Loss* (Jan. 2006). She is one of the writers of younger generation.

Salman Rushdie is pre-eminently concerned with the treatment of history and religion. His *Midnight's Children* (1980) ushers in a new era of fictional art; it is a postmodern novel which reveals "the unreliability of historical discourse."[11] In this novel, the protagonist Saleem Sinai is presented as a troubled and fragmented soul. He suffers from a sense of identity crisis, and the harrowing tale of Mother India during the days of partition becomes his own. Rushdie's novel, *Shame* (1983), portrays the troubled and violent political situation in Pakistan. His *Satanic Verses* (1988) is a novel that has stirred a hornet's nest and has been banned in many Muslim countries, even in India, Pakistan and South Africa.

Vikram Seth is a stupendous diasporic writer who has demonstrated his expertise in both prose and poetry. He began with prose and then shifted to poetry. His travel book, *From Heaven Lake*, and poetical collection entitled *The Humble Administrator's Garden* both appeared in 1983, followed by *The Golden Gate* (1986), *All You Who Sleep Tonight* (1990), and *Beastly Tales from Here and There* (1992), and *A Suitable Boy* (1993). If *The Golden Gate* is a *tour de force* in poetic form, *A Suitable Boy* is one of the longest novels in world literature. It runs into nearly fourteen hundred pages and has earned for Seth the title of "a new Tolstoy".[12] Seth draws upon his rich Indian experience in writing this novel (which is set in the land of his birth).

V.S. Naipaul, the winner of the Nobel Prize for literature in 2001, tried in his writings to revive his connections with the past. He is separated from India by two generations—it was his grandfather who had left India for Trinidad. From the West Indies, Naipaul shifted to England for his residence. Thus, he is "sufficiently removed in both time and space"[13] from India. His three travel books—*An Area of Darkness* (1964), *India: A Wounded Civilization* (1977), and *India: A Million Mutinies* (1991)—are directly based on his visits to India and on his perceptions and experiences here. In them, as also in his novels, there is an acute sense of anxiety born of displacement. Naipaul remarks in his novel *A House for Mr. Biswas* (1961) thus: "Mr. Biswas found it easy to imagine the other race of Indians moving about this road before the world grew dark for them."[14]

Like Naipaul, Nirad Chaudhuri is also critical of and apathetic towards India. Based in London, Chaudhuri burst upon the Indian literary scene with the publication of *The Autobiography of an Unknown Indian* (1951). But more than a personal history, it is a national history in a distorted colour. Whether one agrees with his views on Indian history and civilization is a different matter, but he is "probably India's finest living writer of English prose."[15] Apparently, he suffers from a colonial hang-over and shows extra fidelity towards the erstwhile masters of India. This attitude of his persists in his other works too—*A Passage to England* (1959), *The Continent of Circé* (1966), *To Live or Not to Live* (1971), etc.

Amitav Ghosh has also lived long in England, Egypt and America. For him, globalization (or, moving across the national frontiers) is "an everyday fact of existence."[16] He seems to believe in *The Shadow Lines* (1988) that the national boundaries are merely 'political fictions'. He has written more than half a dozen novels of importance, including *The Circle of Reason* (1986), *The Calcutta Chromosome* (1996) and *Sea of Poppies* (2008). In his novels, Amitav remains a wandering internationalist, disowning the theory of cultural centrality—that 'a culture is rooted in a single place.' In 2018, he earned the prestigious Gyanpeeth national award.

Ved Mehta (born 1934) is a notable diasporic writer who migrated to the U.S.A. from Bombay. He became blind at the age of three, and yet he writes with an acute sense of reality around him. If his autobiography, *Face to Face* (1957), brings out his own perceptions and experiences of life, in most of his other prose works he projects the image of India and her people, their customs and rituals, in an absorbing manner. He nostalgically recalls his past associations with India, with his relatives and friends, in such works as *The New India* (1978), *Mamaji* (1979), and *The Photographs of Chachaji* (1982).

Of all the Indian English poets, A.K. Ramanujan (1929-93) occupies a place of pride. Since the very beginning of the sixties, he had been living in the U.S.A., where he was a Professor of Linguistics at the University of Chicago. In his lifetime he had published three volumes of poetry—*The Striders* (1966), *Relations* (1971), and *Second Sight* (1986). His fourth volume appeared posthumously in 1995 under the caption, *The Black Hen*. Ramanujan has also produced some laudable works of translation (e.g., *The Interior Landscape*, 1967; *Speaking of Siva*, 1972; *Samskara*, 1976; *Poems of Love and War*, 1985; etc.). Recalling his days in India, Ramanujan remarks as follows: "But living/ among relations/ binds the feet" (*Relations*, n.p.). Speaking highly of him, Susanne & Lloyd Rudolph have commented thus: "A polymath; a demanding scholar with demanding standards; a teller of tales, a mesmerizing poet."[17]

The above survey of the old generation of diasporic writers clearly displays that they have lived long or 'too long' in the

West and that they are generally scattered in the whole world—in England, America, Canada and West Indies in particular. The countrywide distribution or dispersion of the writers of Indian diaspora is as follows: Kamala Markandaya, Anita Desai, Salman Rushdie, Vikram Seth, Amitav Ghosh are Britain-based. Even V.S. Naipaul was settled in England; he was a twice-removed author who had shifted to England from Trinidad (West-Indies). Similarly, B. Rajan has migrated to Canada from England, and in both the places he worked as Professor of English. Santha Rama Rau and Bharati Mukherjee have been living in the United States of America.

After England, Canada has immensely attracted the diasporic writers. Since long Saros Cowasjee has taken his residence in Canada. He published his novel, *Goodbye to Elsa*, in 1974, and in it, the protagonist Tristan, the one-eyed man, runs away from his heavyweight wife, Elsa Harbour (of 180 pounds), and one-year old son. He gets entangled with diverse women like Jane, Lydia, Heather Malleson, Marie and Marion, and in a mood of frustration tries to kill himself, bidding 'goodbye' to his wife. Cowasjee makes some witty remarks about persons and places in this novel. Thus, he once makes Tristan to observe: "Besides, the Canadians are so neutral: they are neither sane nor insane, good nor bad. They generally take the colour from their surroundings."[18] The writer shows his concern here for the sovereign nationality and identity of Canada: "We have to be on the guard all the time against the Americanisation of Canada. It is a matter of preserving our Canadian identity."[19]

Like Cowasjee, Cyril Dabydeen is an old settler in Canada. He is also twice-removed geographically; his grandfather, an indentured labourer, had moved from India to Guyana (West Indies), where this author was born, and in 1970 he [Cyril] shifted from Guyana to Canada. He is "one of the most prolific writers",[20] being both poet and novelist. He has about 20 books to his credit. *Poems in Recession* (1972) is his first volume of poems, and it was followed by *Goatsong* (1977), *Heart's Frame* (1979), *Dark Swirl* (1988), *Coastland* (1989), *Berbice Crossing* (1996), and *Black Jesus & Other Stories* (1996—all story-books). Cyril Dabydeen has paid visits to India, first time in 1987.

Other diasporic writers who have gone over to Canada and settled there are of relatively younger generation. Besides Tilottama Rajan who has already been referred to, Uma Parameswaran, Ashish Gupta, Rohinton Mistry, Neil Bissoondath, and M.G. Vassanji, are to be mentioned in this connection. Of these writers, Uma Parameswaran is a Professor of English at the University of Winnipeg, and she has done some commendable creative work. She burst on the literary scene with her book of poems, *Cyclic Hope Cyclic Pain,* in 1973. The volume consists of barely nine poems and a dance-drama entitled "Meera". Poems are simply numbered (no title is given), and "Meera" contains five short scenes related to the life of Meera, who is portrayed here as "a handmaid of Lord Krishna now and forever."[21] Uma has also written another dance-drama called "Sita's Promise" (1981) wherein Sita is depicted as delicate and childlike. Rama suspects her ability to be the Queen of Ayodhaya, but Lakshman defends her and even blames Rama for neglecting the call of love for the sake of duty. The portrayal of these characters in a new light shows Uma Parameswaran's "expatriate sensibility" that has effected "a dynamic act of remythologisation."[22] Parameswaran has also written (*Trishanku* 1987), a series of monologues spoken by various personae, highlighting a sense of alienation, rootlessness and nostalgia in the lives of Savitri Bhave and her husband Sharad, who hail from Ahmedabad and are now settled in Canada. The book of poems, however, ends on a note of reconciliation between the wife and the husband, signalling a tension-free future for their children.

Ashish Gupta, who went to America and then to Canada from Patna, has made a mark in diasporic writing with his two novels, *Dying Traditions* (1992) and *The Toymaker from Wiesbaden* (1993). Rohinton Mistry is another such writer of power and pulse, having published remarkable works like *Tales from Firozshah Baag* (1987), *Such a Long Journey* (1991), *A Fine Balance* (1996), and *Family Matters* (2001). An East Indian who migrated to Canada from the Caribbean, Neil Bissoondath claims to be a 'Canadian Writer.' He has published two collections of short stories, *Digging Up the Mountain* (1985) and *On the Eve of Uncertain Tomorrows* (1990), and two novels, *A Casual Brutality* (1988) and *The Innocence of Age* (1992). Also, M.G. Vassanji has created ripples in the literary world by his modernistic work, *No New Land* (1992), and experimental novel, *The Book of Secrets* (1995).

Two of the younger writers based in Britain are: Pico Iyer and Gita Mehta. Iyer's parents had shifted to London from Bombay, and Iyer was born in Oxford in 1957. Iyer keeps moving from England to Japan and to Cuba, as a result of which he produced two travelogues, a memoir set in Japan (*The Lady and the Monk*, 1991), and a novel located in Cuba (*Cuba and the Night,* 1995), and numerous essays. As for Gita Mehta, she has shot into fame with her novel, *A River Sutra* (1993) where the journey motif is so dominant. Mehta's novel is comparable to Kipling's *Kim* (1901) for employing the theme of search for a mythic river.

The U.S.A. houses Chitra Banerjee Divakaruni, Meena Alexander and Jhumpa Lahiri as diasporic writers of younger generation. Chitra has produced *The Mistress of Spices* (1997), which is a story of Tilo. And Meena has published three books of poetry from W.W. and many other poetry books from America. and a memoir called *Fault Lines* (1993). Jhumpa Lahiri has become so popular with her first collection of short stories, *Interpreter of Maladies* (1999), which won for her the coveted Pulitzer Prize in 2000. Her other works are: *The Namesake* (2003), *Unaccustomed Earth* (2008), *The Lowland* (2013), *Only Goodness* (2013), *Hell-Heaven* (2015), *In Other Words* (2015), and *The Clothing of Books* (2016). In the matter of winning the Pulitzer Prize for her first book, Lahiri is comparable to Arundhati Roy who bagged the Booker Prize for her novel, *The God of Small Things* (1997). The blurb describes Lahiri's book containing nine stories *in toto* thus: "Jhumpa Lahiri's elegant stories tell the lives of Indians in exile, of people navigating between the strict traditions they've inherited and the baffling New World they must encounter every day."[23]

By now, I have mentioned about two dozens of important diasporic writers. I shall mention here two more writers before closing the account, and they are: Sujata Bhatt, who is living in Germany, and Mena Abdullah, who is a Punjabi migrant to Australia. Sujata and Mena represent the Indian diaspora focusing on the disturbing sense of dislocation in their writings. Their expatriate sensibility is effectively expressed in what

Meena Alexander calls "a shifting frame of reference, of multiple worlds,"[24] which characterizes the postcolonial situation. Sujata's collections of poems are: *Brunizem* (1986), *Point No Point* (1997), *Monkey Shadows* (1991), *The Stinking Rose* (1995), *Augatora* (2000), *A Colour for Solitude* (2003), *Pure Lizard* (2008), and *Collected Poems* (2013). Mena's book of short stories, *Time of the Peacock* (1965—written with Ray Mathew), clearly reflects the 'shifting frame of reference'.

To conclude, the above account of the diasporic writings in English convinces us that the Indian immigrants and expatriates have produced a rich harvest of literature in multiple forms and genres, in diverse attitudes and backgrounds. The diasporic writers are settled abroad in different countries—in Britain, Canada, America, Germany, Australia, and the West Indies. They belong to both old and young generations. Their writings bring to the fore their awareness of geographical dislocation, cultural ambivalence, social and political alienation, and absence of centrality. Memory and nostalgia connect them with their homeland and past associations, which feed their imagination to churn out something 'new and strange'.

Notes

1. A.L. McLeod, "Preface", *The Literature of the Indian Diaspora* (New Delhi: Sterling Publishers Pvt. Ltd., 2000), p. ix.
2. Jasbir Jain, "Introduction", *Writers of the Indian Diaspora* (Jaipur & New Delhi: Rawat Publications, 1998), p. 12.
3. Edward Said, *Orientalism* (London: Routledge, 1978), p. 12.
4. *Ibid*., p. 36.
5. See Gayatri Chakravorty Spivak, "Can the Subaltern Speak?" in Gay Nelson and Lawrence Grossberg, eds. *Marxism and the Interpretation of Culture* (London: Macmillan, 1998).
6. Homi Bhabha, *The Location of Culture* (London & New York: Routledge, 1994), p. 177.
7. K.R. Srinivasa Iyengar, *Indian Writing in English*, 4th revised & enlarged edition (New Delhi: Sterling Publishers Pvt. Ltd., 1984), p. 30.
8. A.N. Dwivedi, "Indian Fiction in English: Retrospect and Prospect", *Studies in Contemporary Indian Fiction in English* (Allahabad: Kitab Mahal, 1987), p. 10.

9. S.K. Desai, *Santha Rama Rau* (New Delhi: Arnold-Heinemann, 1976), p. 10.
10. K.T. Sunitha, "Cross-Cultural Dilemmas of Indian Women in Bharati Mukherjee's Fiction", *The Literature of the Indian Diaspora*, ed., A.L. McLeod (2000), p. 263.
11. Alan Lindsay, "Salman Rushdie, History, and the Contemporary Novel", *The Literature of the Indian Diaspora,* ed., McLeod, p. 170.
12. See the Editorial Note in *Recent Indian Fiction*, ed. R.S. Pathak (New Delhi: Prestige Books, 1994), p. 70.
13. Graham Huggan, "Frustration and Fraudulence: V.S. Naipaul's India", *The Literature of the Indian Diaspora*, ed. McLeod, p. 136.
14. V.S. Naipaul, *A House for Mr. Biswas* (London: Andre Deutsch, (1961), p. 397.
15. S.C. Harrex, *The Fire and the Offering,* Vol. I (Calcutta: Writers Workshop, 1977), p. 22.
16. John Thieme, "The Discoverer Discovered: Amitav Ghosh's *The Calcutta Chromosome*", *The Literature of the Indian Diaspora*, ed. McLeod (2000), p. 274.
17. Susanne & Lloyd Rudolph, "Remembering Raman", *The Times of India*, 25 July 1993, p. 8.
18. Saros Cowasjee, *Goodbye to Elsa* (London, Sidney & Toronto: The Bodley Head, 1974), p. 142.
19. *Ibid.*, p. 117.
20. A.L. McLeod, "Cyril Dabydeen: Remembrance of Things Indian", *The Literature of the Indian Diaspora* (2000), p. 189.
21. Uma Parameswaran, *Cyclic Hope Cyclic Pain* (Calcutta: Writers Workshop, 1973), p. 15.
22. Jancy James, "Remythologizing as Expatriate Vision and Art: An Intertextual Reading of Uma Parameswaran's *Sita's Promise* and *Meera", Writers of the Indian Diaspora*, ed. Jasbir Jain (1998), p. 203.
23. Quoted from the blurb of *Interpreter of Maladies* (New Delhi: HarperCollins Publishers India, 1999).
24. Meena Alexander, "Freedom and the Indian Diaspora: An Interview", *The Hindu Literary Review* (Chennai, 21 December 1997), p. 3.

3

New English Literatures of the Colonized

I

New Literatures in English in the postcolonial period definitely mark a break with the past, in terms of experience and application, in the areas of language and culture—the past which was dominated by the Empire and its 'vaulting ambition' (to use a Shakespearean expression). These literatures have shown to the world that the process of decolonization has now begun and the erstwhile subject nations are paying back to the European masters in their own coin by writing new English Literatures in an altered shade of language and culture. Even history of the subject-nation is getting reshaped.

Frantz Fanon drew our attention to the miserable conditions of subject-nations and their peoples as 'the Wretched of the Earth' who must rewrite their history—"The Third World must start over a new history of man" (1961: 238)—because the European Empire has given us nothing but "the racial hatred, slavery, exploitation and above all, the bloodless genocide whereby one and a half billion men have been written off" (*Ibid.*). Fanon gave a clarion call to the Third World, in a mood of anger and revolt, in his two thought-provoking books *Black Skin, White Masks* (1952) and *The Wretched of the Earth* (1961) written in background of the anti-colonial Algerian war of liberation against the repressive colonial power of France, to rise above the Empire's black design of letting loose a rein of "psychological terror, cultural arrogance and even physical torture," as Homi Bhabha puts it in his excellent Foreword to *The Wretched of the Earth* (2004, ed., xi). Obviously, in this most quoted, and quarreled over, book, Fanon powerfully articulates his ethics and politics of a decolonization when he says, "The last shall be the first" (1961 and 2004: 2 & 3), and recognizes the inevitability of the upsurge of violence in society or nation-state—"the almighty body of violence rearing up in reaction to the primary violence of the colonizer" (50). Fanon believes that decolonization is "always a violent event" (1), and that it arises with national liberation, with the rise of a new nation-state and with its establishment of diplomatic relations and economic ties with the Empire that had earlier subjugated it. Though Bhabha has associated 'decolonization' with 'globalization' (xi-xii) and with 'global cosmopolitanism' (1994: xiv), Fanon links it with the change of the world-order by creating a condition of total disorder (2). Fanon adds further: "Decolonization, we know, is a historical process" (2), and it is "the encounter between two congenitally antagonistic forces" (2) represented by the colonist and the colonized. The colonist derives his validity, i.e., his wealth, from the colonial system. Decolonization produces a new generation of men, endowed with a new language and literature. Fanon thinks that "Decolonization is truly the creation of new men" (2), and that it implies "the urgent need to thoroughly change the colonial situation" (2). New literary forms and contents are, as a result, created by the liberated new men (who can be precisely called 'the decolonized'). This is what Rajeev S. Patke means when he remarks that "Postcolonial literary traditions in English are linked by a number of shared features, chief among them, the challenges of putting various forms of English to local use, answering local needs" (2006 and 2007: 238).

Another book of great significance from the viewpoint of our discussion is *The Empire Writes Back* (1989) by Bill Ashcroft, Gareth Griffiths and Helen Tiffin. In this book, as Salman Rushdie puts it, "...the Empire writes back to the Centre..." (quoted from the outer cover of the book). It debates about the deplorable relationship of the colonizer and the colonized and investigates the powerful forces acting on language and literature of the postcolonial era. It offers a radical critique of Eurocentric notions of literature and language, and mentions a number of countries which are producing new literatures in English, such countries as Australia, New Zealand, Canada, the Caribbean countries, India, Pakistan, African countries, Bangladesh, Sri Lanka, Malaysia, Malta, Singapore and South Pacific Islands (1989: 2). Even the literature of the USA can be placed in this category, but because of its current position of superpower, and the neo-colonizing role it has played, its post-colonial status has been overlooked. The authors of *The Empire Writes Back* maintain that the study of English has always been a densely political and cultural phenomenon, and that the emergence of English as an academic discipline goes with the expansion of imperialism (2-3). Obviously, new literatures in English are post-colonial literatures being written presently by the authors of the erstwhile colonized countries, and these authors are interpreting the history and culture of their respective countries with a patriotic zeal. For them, the colonized is no less important than the Centre. The Centre is rather forced today to accept their thoughts and writings in "a process of incorporation" (7). By way of conclusion, *The Empire Writes Back* makes certain observations which are quite valid and tenable today. One of its observations is:

> The contemporary art, philosophy, and literature produced by post-colonial societies are in no sense contributions or simple adaptations of European models.... Indeed, the process of cultural decolonization has involved a radical dismantling of the European codes and a post-colonial subversion and appropriation of the dominant European discourses. (1989: 220)

This observation obviously lays emphasis on 'a radical dismantling' of the European codes and discourses to help facilitate the process of cultural decolonization. Secondly, postcolonial culture is "inevitably a hybridized phenomenon involving a dialectical relationship between the 'grafted' European cultural systems and an indigenous ontology with its impulse to create or recreate an independent local identity" (220). In constructing or reconstructing such an independent local identity, it is not possible to return to or to rediscover 'an absolute pre-colonial cultural purity', nor is it possible to create national or regional formations entirely independent of their historical connections with the European colonial power. It is so because there exists "a dynamic interaction between European hegemonic systems and 'peripheral' subversions of them" (220). Bill Ashcroft and his co-authors uphold the view that postcolonial literatures/ cultures "are constituted in counter-discursive rather than homologous practices" (221). They conclude their discussions of the postcolonial upsurge of new literatures *vis-à-vis* the future of English studies by pointing out three things: (1) "The concept of a standard English has been exploded", (2) As a further implication of this decentering, "the English canon is radically reduced within a new paradigm of international english [sic] studies", and (3) The concept of literary studies in general will be revitalized by the perception of the complexities of postcolonial texts (221-22).

II

We have analyzed above the two seminal works on colonialism and postcolonialism, and the process of decolonization started by the erstwhile colonized but now liberated intellectuals/authors who are presently dismantling and recoding the European/ English canon. Such authors are, in a way, challenging the West-dominated discourses in their writings and raising the questions of European hegemony in their texts. Their voice is the voice of revolt and resistance, aiming at the transformation of dominant discourses of their previous masters.

It is not possible here, in a short space, to review or analyse the new literatures of all the colonized countries/peoples (as mentioned earlier while discussing *The Empire Writers Back*). At the most, we are to take stock of new English literatures of such countries as Africa, Australia, New Zealand, Canada, the West Indies, and India, for shortage of time and space.

For one thing, we have left out new literatures of America, South or Southeast Asia, and South Pacific Islands for the reasons specified above. Before entering into a discussion of new literatures in the six chosen countries which experienced the trauma of colonization in one or the other form and in a particular period of history, it is in place to mention here that the Americans were the first to break free from British colonizers. With the declaration of American Independence in July 1776 and later with the rise of America as a world-power in the political arena, America has wiped off the tag of being a colonized country. The American history as a nation, its powerful language and literature, its military strength and political leadership have all combined to enable it "to avoid the appellation of 'postcolonial'," as Rajeev S. Patke has remarked (2006 and 2007: 238). Noah Webster had prepared the background for it by setting an American standard for language as early as 1789, and the *American Spelling Book* (1783) was selling like a hot cake in the US market (a million copies a year by the 1850s). Emerson's essays and poems, H.D. Thoreau's *Walden Pond* (1854), Whiteman's *Leaves of Grass* (1855), Emily Dickinson's verses and mystical songs and Hawthorne's *The Scarlet Letter* (1850), Herman Melville's *Moby Dick* (1851) and H.W. Longfellow's lyrics consolidated American Literature in the nineteenth century. After that, in the twentieth century, Robert Frost (who was awarded the Pulitzer Prize four times), Ernest Hemingway (who won the Nobel Prize for Literature in 1954 on his novel, The *Old Man and the Sea*, 1952), Saul Bellow (who earned the Nobel Prize in 1976), Philip Roth, Sylvia Plath, Anne Sexton, Ezra Pound, T.S. Eliot, Wallace Stevens, E.E. Cummings, William Carlos Williams, Eugene O'Neill, and Arthur Miller have made substantive literary contributions.

III

After a brief consideration of new American Literature, to which the nomenclature of 'postcolonial' is usually not applied, we pass on to the new literatures of 'postcolonial' countries proper, such as Africa/South Africa, the secular countries like Australia, New Zealand and Canada and then the Caribbean, and India, and review how far they have gone in rewriting the colonial history and revitalizing their native tradition and culture.

First of all, let us examine Africa/South Africa in this context. The African continent witnessed a flourishing slave trade; the Portuguese and the Spanish came first, followed by the British, the Dutch, and the French, who occupied the western parts of Africa, which later became the nations of Liberia and Sierra Leone. Slaves freed from North America were also shipped back and settled along the Atlantic coast (i.e., western coast) of Africa. The black skin and negritude of the transported slaves are the recognizable traits of new African literature. Speaking about the black African people, one of the Senegalese poets called Leopold Senghor (1906-2001) reeling under the French control writes thus:

> They call us men of cotton, coffee and oil.
> They call us men of death.
> But we are men of dance, whose feet get stronger
> As we pound upon firm earth.
>
> (The *Collected Poetry*, trans. M. Dixon. Charlottesvilla, London: UP of Virginia, 1991, p. 14).

This sort of utterances led to the freedom of the French colonies first, followed by the British colonies in West Africa, beginning with Ghana in 1957 where, after a series of military coups, parliamentary democracy was restored in 2001. Nigeria, the most populous region of Africa, gained independence in 1960 and became a republic in 1963. Soon, its three culturally distinct communities—the Hausa, the Yoruba, and the Gybo—were engaged in a civil war (1967-70) which ended with the restoration of parliamentary government in 1999 after sixteen years of military rule. Similarly, freedom came to East Africa in the early 1960s—to countries like Tanganyika (in 1961), to Zanzibar (in 1963), to Uganda (in 1962), and to Kenya (in 1963). Under the leadership of Kenneth Kaunda, Zambia opposed apartheid in neighbouring South Africa, but the economic crisis ended his rule in 1992. Another country, Malawi, under the rule of Hastings Banda, continued its ties with the apartheid South Africa up to 1993. In South Africa, the white minority rule ran from 1948 up to the early 1990s. Earlier, Mahatma Gandhi had opposed the racial rule in South Africa and later on Nelson Mandela waged a fight there against the minority white government. Since 1934, South Africa has been following the path of multi-racial democracy. Most of the African countries retained English as the national language and the media of instruction in universities (R.S. Patke, 2006 and 2007: 108).

Some of the stalwarts of new African writing, who stressed the need of decolonizing literature and culture, were Chinua Achebe, Ben Okri, Wole Soyinka, Ngugi wa Thiong, Nadine Gordimer, and J.M. Coetzee. Achebe's *Things Fall Apart* (1958) is possibly the best-known African novel of the twentieth century. Okri blends fantasy and reality in his novel *The Famished Road* (1991). Here the spiritual and real worlds coalesce to form a powerful narrative. Wole Soyinka, a prolific writer of prose, poetry and drama, shot into limelight in 1993 with his Nobel Prize winning work, Nadine Gardiner became so popular with the novel *July's People* which was awarded the Nobel Prize for Literature in 1991. It seriously reflects on the imagined conditions of the post-independent South Africa. J.M. Coetzee also won the coveted Nobel Prize for Literature in 2003 for his *Life and Times of Michael K*, a story with a blurred hero and a vague historical and geographical background Nadine Gardiner, who was a while novelist of South Africa, rightly surmised that "black writers have had to look for survival away from the explicit... to the implicit; and in their case they have turned instinctively to poetry" (quoted from Patke, 113). The socio-political slant of black African writing stirred poets like Mtshali in the 1970s, Kunen and Don Mattera in the 1980s, to come out with powerful patriotic songs.

IV

Now is the turn of the new Caribbean literature. Due to the atrocities of the European colonizers, the Caribbean people encountered "the worst features of colonialism" which included:

> The virtual annihilation of the native population of Caribs and Arawaks; the plundering and internecine piracy amongst the European powers; the deracination and atrocities of the slave trade and plantation slavery, and the subsequent systems of indenture.... (Bill Ashcroft *et al.*, 1989: 144)

In the early days of slavery, cultural clash, linguistic dilemma, and miscegenation constituted "the brutal texture of Caribbean life" (*Ibid.*, 144). Race and ancestry were issues of supreme importance in the Caribbean history. British educational policy deliberately excluded any mention of slavery in the West Indies or of the African ancestry of the slaves. The noted poet and critic, Edward Kamau Brathwaite, propounds the theory of 'creolization' to describe the history and culture of the Caribbean. Though he does not dismiss its African or Amerindian connection, he lays emphasis on "the European presence in Creolization" (Ashcroft *et al.*, 146). Like Brathwaite, Dennis Williams accepts the role of cross-culturality, language and landscape as the paramount conditions of the colonial situation. Dennis Williams proposes a theory of art, keeping in mind the Guyanese society, which is based on the image of post-colonial 'catalysis' (*i.e.*, the importance attached to the creative meaning of the present for the individual). Williams thinks that Wilson Harris is the supreme practitioner of the Caribbean catalysis.

Wilson Harris is a powerful creative writer and theorist of the West Indies. He has written two books of poetry, eighteen novels, two volumes of short stories, several articles, and two volumes of literary theory titled *Tradition, the Writer and Society* (1967) and *The Womb of Space: The Cross-Cultural Imagination* (1983). In his works, Harris believes in "psychic regeneration through catastrophe" (Ashcroft, *et al.*, 148), "in the transforming powers...of the imagination" (149) which can retrieve "the lost" (149). He also believes in "the very energy involved in violent and destructive acts" leading to "the seeds of creativity" (149). Like Williams, Harris maintains that the racially mixed population of the Caribbean, particularly Guyana, provides possibilities for "cross-cultural creativity" as well as for "de-imperialization of apparently monolithic European forms, ontologies and epistemologies" (*Ibid.,* 151).

The Caribbean literature got a shot in the arm in the 1950s. In September 1956, the first Congress of Negro Writers and Artists was organised here. Earlier, in the 1940s, the BBC radio programme had launched "Caribbean Voices" providing opportunities to the West Indies writers and artists. Some of the writers even got a chance to be published from the UK, such writers as John Hearne, Samuel Selvon, V.S. Naipaul, and George Lamming. Many of these writers were searching for roots and locating identity, and they largely wrote on issues of race, culture, language and landscape. Since 1960 when Saint-John Perse was awarded the Nobel Prize for Literature, the Caribbean authors and their works have been getting international recognition for their literary worth. In this respect, the two creative stalwarts must be mentioned—Derek Walcott and V.S. Naipaul—who won the coveted Nobel Prize for Literature in 1992 and 2002 respectively. Through their writings, they have raised the voice of their people against all forms of tyranny and exploitation which were rampant in the colonial days.

V

We now turn to the new Australian literature. At the very outset, it must be pointed out that the better colonies like Australia, New Zealand and Canada (America being excluded) strove to establish their 'indigeneity', keeping it apart from their sense of a continuing European inheritance. Bill Ashcroft and his co-authors are of the view that "...their situation differs from that of Indians or Africans whose problem was to retrieve or reconstruct their culture at the end of a period of foreign rule" (1989: 134). Australian authors have largely written about such themes as aboriginality, egalitarianism, democracy, national identity, migration, geographical borders, the sea-adventures, the complexities of urban living, and the 'beauty and the terror' of life in the Australian bush. Some of the well-known Australian writers are: Patrick White (who won the Nobel Prize for Literature in 1973 for her novel), Christina Stead, David Malouf, A.D. Hope, Judith Wright (A confessional poet), Peter Carey, Broadley Trever, and Marcus Clarke. In the Australian writings, as a whole, there are two elements—the imported and the indigenous. P.R. Stephensen in his essay "The Foundations of Culture in Australia" also supports this idea.

New Zealand enjoys the same native privileges and imported cultural inheritance as Australia, and as a settler colony, New Zealand found itself in a welter of confusion when it was confronted with the choice of language and culture. The early settlers of New Zealand discovered themselves as 'beleaguered victims' betrayed by fate. R.A.K. Mason (1905-71) in his "Sonnet of Brotherhood" depicts them so:

here in this far-pitched perilous hostile place
this solitary hard-assaulted spot
fixed at the friendless outer edge of space.

(Cited in Rajeev S. Patke, 134)

The above passage shows that even the poets were aware of their predicament—how to relate the local to the universal. A. Curnow, a New Zealand critic of the twentieth century, has done a commendable job by editing the two anthologies, *A Book of New Zealand Verse* (1945) and *The Penguin Book of New Zealand Verse* (1960). No doubt, Curnow emphasized that "a truly indigenous literature would be regional and nationalist", but the younger modern poets of New Zealand were for giving it an international character. And new poets like Charles Brasch, Dennis Glover, and Bill Manhire came out of the traditional poetry of rocks and hills, and yet continued the application of the Maori language with newer idioms. Writers like Patricia Grace and Witi Ihimaera are the glaring examples of it.

As regards Canada, a country of "dual origin and official bilingualism", as suggested by Hari Mohan Prasad in an article (*IJES*, 2016: 7), it welcomes immigrants from different nations and cultures. To a large extent, new literature in Canada strives to discover a personal and national identity. The well-known literary critic, Northrop Frye, rightly points out that the overwhelming question before the Canadian writer has been: 'Where is here?' Definitely a host of writers have enriched the Canadian literature, and some of the notable ones are: Margaret Atwood, Margaret Laurence, Gabrielle Roy and Carol Shields, and Alice Munro (who won the Nobel Prize for Literature). These writers as well as some Indian authors having settled in Canada since long, such as B. Rajan, Saros Cowasjee, Uma Parameswaran, and Rohinton Mistry, have done a lot to raise new Canadian literature to the international level.

VI

Lastly, we take up the case of India which has also witnessed the worst conditions of colonization during British rule in this land. New English literature may well begin after India's independence in August 1947. R.K. Narayan, Mulk Raj Anand,

Raja Rao in fiction and P. Lal, Nissim Ezekiel, Kamala Das and A.K. Ramanujan in poetry are credited to have ushered in a new era of writing, marking a break with the past and heralding the dawn of decolonized literature in Indian English.

In fact, India has got a long critical tradition, beginning with the *Natyashastra* of Bharata Muni (C. 200 B.C.). Sanskrit aestheticians like Vishwanath, Mammat, Anandavardhan and Pt. Jagannath have made minute and sound commentaries and evolved 'highly sophisticated theories' that can be applied in the evaluation of works of art. Because of them we are compelled today to reconsider the use of western critical terms/tools in assessing a literary work of Indian origin and or to apply such terms/tools of an established Sanskrit tradition as 'rasa', 'dhvani', 'alankara', 'rupak' and 'vakrokti' (irony) in our critical evaluations. Critics like Krishna Rayan (1984) and K. Krishnamoorthy (1984) are of the firm view that indigenous terms/tools are more appropriate in the assessment of contemporary literatures in Indian vernacular languages, including those in Tamil and Kannada, than the imported terms/tools. And this kind of assessment is definitely a step towards 'decolonization'. Bill Ashcroft and his co-authors support this argument when they observe that "the traditional aesthetic and its concepts to modern literatures...may well be a powerful tool for opening up the distinctive features of contemporary Indian texts subsumed under imported critical and generic assumptions" (117). As suggested by Ashcroft and others, the *rasa-dhvani* theory (i.e., the emotion or aesthetic pleasure and suggestion theory) being applied to Indian texts will prove a potent theory to deconstruct and then to reconstruct the old parameters/codes/canons idolized and perpetrated by British rulers.

Of all the poets, R. Parthasarathy is nearer the truth when he hints at the process of decolonization in the following lines:

> My tongue in English chains.
> I return, after a generation to you.
> I am at the end
> of my Dravidic tether,
> hunger for you unassuaged.
> I falter, stumble. (1976: 44)

Parthasarathy is pleading here powerfully for a return to writing in Tamil after writing in English. He deplores that so long he has been 'whoring after English gods', but now he wants to discover the past and return to Tamil, his mother tongue. Two women poets—Kamala Das (1934-2008) and Sujata Bhatt (born 1956)—come to my mind as far as the use of English as a medium of expression is concerned. Mrs. Das is very eloquent about her own choice of language, and says in her poem "An Introduction":

> ...I am Indian, very brown, born in
> Malabar. I speak three languages, write in
> Two, dream in one. Don't write in English, they said,
> English is not your mother-tongue.

and again:

> The language I speak
> Becomes mine, its distortions, its queerness
> All mine, mine alone. It is half English, half
> Indian, funny perhaps, but it is honest.
> It is as human as I am human....
>
> (*The Old Playhouse*.... 1973: 27)

Kamala Das is clearly speaking of the decolonization of English when she points out the distortions and the queerness of Indian English. And Sujata Bhatt in her poem "History is a Broken Narrative" (extracted from *Augatora,* 2000) writes as follows:

> History is a broken narrative
> Where you make your language
> When you change it. (2000: 43)

Mrs. Bhatt is also hinting here at the breaking of history and at the making of new language—the two salient features of decolonization.

In poetry, it was Rabindranath Tagore who made India, nay the whole world, proud of his achievements in literature through his monumental work, *Gitanjali* (1913), which fetched for him the prestigious Nobel Prize for Literature. The content and the form of *Gitanjali* deeply impressed W.B. Yeats, who wrote an excellent Introduction to it. Some other literary luminaries of the past were Henry Derozio, Toru Dutt, Sarojini

Naidu, Harindranath Chattopadhyay, Manmohan Ghosh and Sri Aurobindo. The last-named one could match R.N. Tagore in profundity of thought, sublimity of vision, and sonorousness of utterance. His *Savitri* is a modern epic of Miltonic grace and grandeur. In the post-Independence days, India has produced a number of gifted poets, such as Nissim Ezekiel, P. Lal, Kamala Das, Dom Moraes, A.K. Ramanujan, Pritish Nandy, Jayanta Mahapatra, R. Parthasarathy, Arun Kolatkar, Shiv K. Kumar, and Keki N. Daruwalla who have experimented variously in both content and technique. Some new voices have emerged in Indian English poetry in recent times, and they have tried their best to throw away the colonial hangovers and to enter into a fresh arena of language and culture. Some of these 'new' voices are: Eunice d'Souza, Gauri Deshpande, Niranjan Mohanty, A.N. Dwivedi, Charu Sheel Singh, Sujata Bhatt, and Smita Agarwal.

In the field of Indian English fiction, Indian writers have scaled new heights. The beginnings were made by 'the Big Three' (a phrase coined by William Walsh)—Mulk Raj Anand, R.K. Narayan and Raja Rao—and the *genre* was consolidated by such writers as Bhabani Bhattacharya, Manohar Malgonkar, Kamala Markandaya, Anita Desai, Arun Joshi and Nayantara Sahgal. Quite in recent times, since the 1980's till today, Indian English fiction has made a commendable progress in the hands of V.S. Naipaul, Salman Rushdie, Agha Shahid Ali, Rohinton Mistry, Jhumpa Lahiri, and Kiran Desai (all diasporic writers) and some indigenous writers like Arundhati Roy, Githa Hariharan, Gita Mehta, Aravind Adiga and Chetan Bhagat who are all writing back to the Empire in an emphatic way, experimenting afresh with the history of the nation, its language (-s) and culture (-s), its mode of perception and expression.

Scholars like Bill Ashcroft *et al.* have rightly suggested that there is a rich reservoir of contemporary writing in various vernacular languages of India, and that new literatures being produced today in these vernacular languages (Marathi, Bengali, Tamil, Telugu, Kannada, Malayalam, Sindhi, Punjabi, etc.) far outweigh in quantity and quality the works produced in English (*sic*, 1989; 121). Hindi, our national language, has a remarkable treasure of creative literature, and for its vocabulary and sustenance it largely relies on classical Sanskrit. What is most needed at the moment is an extensive translation of texts from these vernacular languages. Such translations will, on the one hand, enrich our literary and cultural heritage and on the other, quicken the pace of decolonization.

VII

To sum up: New English literatures of the colonized, at best, emerge from the linear development of history in its various stages—from 'the precolonial', to 'the colonial' and to 'the postcolonial'—portraying the unsavoury relationship between the colonizers and the colonized. Then a time comes when the colonized countries and people realize the predicament of their existence under a repressive, tyrannical imperial power. They rise in revolt, offer stiff resistance to the foreign power and eventually break asunder the shackles of slavery and exploitation and attain the long-cherished independence. Writers and artists lend their support and strength to such national struggles for independence and sometimes even go to jails (for example, Mahatma Gandhi, Pt. Jawaharlal Nehru, Maulana Abul Kalam Azad, etc., in the Indian context). And independence introduces changes in their attitudes towards the erstwhile rulers. Their changed attitude is reflected in their subversive use of the imported language and the imposed education and culture. In the foregoing pages, it has been shown *how* this subversion or decolonization is effected in new literatures of Africa/South Africa, the West Indies, and India in a major way, and in those of the settler countries (*i.e.*, Australia, New Zealand and Canada) in a limited manner. As for India, the noted novelist Raja Rao rightly points out that English is "the language of our intellectual make-up...but not of our emotional make-up", and that "we are all instinctively bilingual, many of us writing in our own language and in English. We cannot write like the English. We should not. We cannot write only as Indians. We have grown to look at the large world as part of us" (1938 and 1974: v). Certainly, we have to accept English as a global phenomenon, as an international language, but we as writers and artists must leave our own imprint on it, and that will be our real contribution to the process of its decolonization.

Works Cited

Ashcroft, Bill, Gareth Griffiths and Helen Tiffin, 1989 and 2010. *The Empire Writes Back*. London and New York: Routledge.

Bhabha, Homi K. 2004. "Foreword", *The Wretched of the Earth*. New York: Government Press.

________. 1994. *The Location of Culture*. London and New York: Routledge.

Bhatt, Sujata. 2000. *Augatora*. Manchester: Carcanet.

Das, Kamala. 1973. "An Introduction", *The Old Playhouse and Other Poems*. Madras: Orient Longman.

Fanon, Frantz. 1961 and 2004. *The Wretched of the Earth*. New York: Government Press.

Parthasarathy, R. 1976. *Rough Passage*. New Delhi: Oxford University Press.

Patke, Rajeev S. 2006 and 2007. *Postcolonial Poetry in English*. New Delhi: Oxford University Press.

Prasad, Hari Mohan. 2016. "World Literature in English", *The Indian Journal of English Studies*, L. III, 1-11.

Rao, Raja. 1938 and 1974. "Foreword", *Kanthapura*. Madras: Oxford University Press.

Tagore, Rabindranath. 1913. *Gitanjali*. London: Macmillan and Co.

Walsh, William. 1976. "The Big Three", *Indian Writing in English*, ed. Ramesh Mohan. Madras: Orient Longman.

Yeats, W.B. 1913. "Introduction", *Gitanjali*. London: Macmillan and Co.

4

T.S. Eliot's Criticism and the Great English Romantics: A Comparative View

T.S. Eliot and the great English Romantics—Wordsworth, Coleridge, Shelley, and Keats (with the exception of Byron, who was not a conscious critic)—share the literary platform in regard to certain doctrinal issues involved despite their professed divergences—Eliot being a 'classicist' while the Romantics being in the opposite camp. They arrive at identical formulations concerning their critical concepts of 'impersonality' or 'objectivity', 'objective correlative' or 'negative capability', theory of poetic diction ('music' being the prime concern of both), 'unified' or 'organic' sensibility, and the 'social function' of poetry. No doubt, Eliot approached the Romantics with a good deal of caution lest his own concepts of poetry should be contradicted. Moreover, the early poetry of T.S. Eliot, say up to "The Love Song of J. Alfred Prufrock" (1915), remains largely 'romantic' in vein and style,[1] though it may sound a little fallacious. Today, even doctoral theses are being written on this aspect of Eliot's art and mind. In his *On Poetry* (1947), Eliot remarks that he wrote *The Waste Land* (1922) to release "his personal emotions" or "the tension in his mind."[2]

Most of Eliot's critical concepts are contained in *The Sacred Wood* (1920), *For Lancelot Andrewes* (1928), *Selected Essays* (1932), *The Use of Poetry and the Use of Criticism* (1933), *Essays Ancient and Modern* (1936), *The Idea of a Christian*

Society (1939), *Notes toward the Definition of Culture* (1948), and *On Poetry and Poets* (1957). These various critical works of Eliot clearly demonstrate that he was on the side of orderliness, objectivity, impersonality, and external authority. He found English criticism "no better than a Sunday park of contending and contentious orators, who have not even arrived at the articulation of their difference."[3] He maintained that English criticism had ever been divided between the conflicting claims of 'classicism' and 'romanticism'. While 'classicism' owes its unflinching allegiance to an external authority, 'romanticism' is devoted to individual liberty. Since the love of liberty is deeply ingrained in English character, 'classicism' has no bright future in England. And yet, he tenaciously stuck to 'classicism', and in 1927 declared that he was a "classicist in literature."[4] This declaration, made somewhat arbitrarily, naturally ranges him against the 'romantics' and their critical credo. But literature can't be science, and Eliot's declaration seems to be only partially true. In truth, Eliot's critical concepts do not totally negate the romantic concepts in several matters, and this certainly bewilders his readers.

Eliot enunciated his 'impersonal theory of poetry' in his seminal essay, "Tradition and the Individual Talent" (1919), which was first included in *The Sacred Wood* (1920) and later in *Selected Essays* (1932). In this essay, Eliot formulated his views of the objectivity of poetry by suggesting that the poet and the poem are two separate things. He took two things for his consideration—"the relation of the poet to the past"[5] and "the relation of the poem to its author."[6] According to Eliot, the past never dies with us; rather it lives in the present. If a poet happens to be truly great and good, he derives a good deal from his ancestors (the dead poets) who "assert their immortality most vigorously."[7] But he does not imitate them slavishly and alters or modifies their works in a perceptible manner. This then becomes a ceaseless affair of 'giving' and 'taking'. While in 'giving' he has to assert his individuality, in 'taking' he has to suppress or subdue it. As the poet has to 'take' from a long line of the illustrious past, he has to undergo "a continual surrender of himself" or "a continual self-sacrifice, a continual extinction of personality."[8]

As such, there is scarcely any connection, whatsoever, between the poet's personality and his poem. In formulating such a theory of poetry, Eliot seems to be opposed to Wordsworth's theory of poetry—that poetry is "the spontaneous overflow of powerful feelings" which are "recollected in tranquility."[9] Eliot has indubitably, though mildly, criticized Wordsworth on this count in the said essay as well as in *The Use of Poetry and the Use of Criticism* (1933).

To my thinking, Wordsworth may not be so devastatingly depersonalised and destabilised in his poetry as Eliot was, but he is also 'objective' and 'impersonal' in his own way, especially when he qualifies his definition of poetry with the phrase "recollected in tranquility". This qualifying phrase goes a long way in rendering Wordsworth 'unromantic' and 'objective'. That's why he has been characterized as a 'classicist' among the Romantics. Like a true classicist, Wordsworth counsels the grieving Laodamia as follows:

> Be taught, O faithful Consort, to control
> Rebellious passion, for the Gods approve
> The depth and not the tumult of the soul....[10]

Just as a good wife controls the turbulence of 'passion'; so, a good poet ought to be balanced and restrained in the articulation of his emotions. But Eliot thought that Wordsworth's definition of poetry was "an inexact formula", for it was "neither emotion, nor recollection, nor, without distortion of meaning, tranquility."[11] Eliot mainly criticized Wordsworth on the ground that he did not render his poetry more 'conscious and deliberate'; he did not question the latter's 'objectivity'. Even S.T. Coleridge, a co-author of the *Lyrical Ballads* (1798), mentions 'objectivity' in Chapter XV of his *Biographia Literaria* (1817), where it is described as a source of manifesting 'genius'—"the utter aloofness of the poet's own feelings...."[12]

Another critical concept of far-reaching significance is found in Eliot's innovative phrase 'objective correlative', which aims at expressing 'emotion' in art-form with perfect 'objectivity'. This phrase occurs in the essay "Hamlet and His Problems" (1919) contained in *The Sacred Wood* (1920) and attempts to explain how 'emotion' is best expressed in poetry. In this connection, Eliot remarks:

> The only way of expressing emotion in the form of art is by finding an "objective correlative"; in other words, a set of objects, a situation, a chain of events which shall be the formula of that *particular* emotion; such that when the external facts, which must terminate in sensory experience, are given, the emotion is immediately evoked.[13]

The poet can't transmit his emotion directly to the reader's mind. What he is required to do is to turn it into something concrete—a picture of person, place, or thing that suggests it—in order to evoke the same emotion in the reader. That 'concrete' thing in which it is embodied is actually its 'objective correlative' or 'external equivalent'. To illustrate his point, Eliot cites the examples of Shakespeare's great tragedies, particularly *Macbeth*, where the highly agonised state of Lady Macbeth's mind is skillfully conveyed to us by merely making her repeat her past actions while walking in her sleep. The unconscious repetition of her past actions is the 'objective correlative' of the present deep agony embedded in her heart. The lack-lustre eyes and the burning taper in her hand merely enhance the over-all impact of objectification (the avowed aim of an artist).

Of the great Romantics, John Keats comes close to Eliot when the former propounds the doctrine of 'negative capability' as essential to poetic practice. This 'capability' enables a poet to keep himself away from the hold of 'irritable reaching after fact and reason'. Keats, a worshipper of 'truth' and 'beauty' in all things and forms, shows glimpses of this capability in his poetic practice, especially in his famous Odes. Thus, "Ode to Indolence" was composed by him in a state of restlessness and uncertainty, generating an aversion to action in him and an escapist tendency too. His "Ode on a Grecian Urn" depicts the pagan and ritualistic Greek life, shorn of all personal details. But Eliot highly admired Keats's "Ode to Psyche" for its inimitable objectivity. In the long poem titled *Lamia* (1819), all the deceptive charms of the serpent-woman disappear at the approach of the philosopher (a person of reason and reality). The noted critic, Douglas Bush, rightly states that *Lamia* portrays "the struggle between passion and the craving to escape from passion".[14] In "Ode to a Nightingale", the poet writes thus:

> That I might drink, and leave the world unseen
> And with thee fade away into the forest dim:[15]

In order to identify himself with the 'object' of his creation, the poet wishes to 'leave the world unseen'. The well-known critic, Graham Hough, judiciously comments that Keats' Odes are truly the "supreme examples of Negative Capability...the Odes are not merely decorative and descriptive poems...."[16] As a poet, Keats was ever concerned with the question of attaining 'objectivity and range' and the critic Edward Lobb aptly suggests that Keats 'felt an uneasiness in fear of losing them'.

Another important critical concept enunciated by Eliot is discovered in 'auditory imagination'. Critics like Helen Gardner and F.O. Matthiessen have each written a chapter while discussing this phrase to emphasize the musical quality of poetry. Eliot praises Chaucer for his 'auditory imagination' which Langland lacked despite his larger imaginative vision of the fourteenth-century life. Miss Gardner, for one, observes about Chaucer as under:

> ....Chaucer's 'divine fluidity', his achievement in creating the English rhetoric line, wedding the noble verse-forms of Italy to the rhythms of English speech, his unerring sense of verbal melody, his skill in the verse paragraph, the range of his vocabulary and his discretion in the use of it, employing the homely and exotic in close juxtaposition, the union in his poetry of grace and strength: all these make him a poet who has in a high degree what Langland lacks: what Mr. Eliot has called 'auditory imagination.'[17]

Spenser also has an ample power to create 'a new music' in his verse, but Arnold is deficient in "the musical qualities of verse."[18] Eliot has thrown sufficient light on 'auditory imagination' in *The Use of Poetry and the Use of Criticism* (1933):

> What I call the 'auditory imagination' is the feeling for syllable and rhythm, penetrating far below the conscious levels of thought and feeling, invigorating every word; sinking to the most primitive and forgotten, returning to the origin and bringing something back, seeking the beginning and the end. It works through meanings,...and

> fuses the old and obliterated and the trite, the current, and the new and surprising, the most ancient and the most civilized mentality.[19]

Each of the *Quartets*, but for "The Dry Salvages", has the final and the fifth movement devoted to the exploration of the mystery of language and the scope of the employment of musical words. Speaking of the 'music of poetry', Eliot writes as follows:

> The music of poetry...must be a music latent in the common speech of its time.[20]

Thus, Eliot's 'auditory imagination' is closely aligned with 'the music of poetry' emanating from 'the common speech'.

The great Romantics also laid an emphasis on the 'music of poetry.' In fact, Coleridge considered it (or, 'musical delight') as a manifestation of 'genius'. In his view, it is to be had in 'the perfect sweetness of versification', in its adaptation to the subject-matter, and in the power of varying the rhythm of words to the requirement of thought.[21] The 'musical delight' in poetry is verily an expression of the music in the poet's soul. Wordsworth and Shelley also display an enviable sense of 'music' in poetry. Wordsworth's Lucy poems and shorter lyrics and Shelley's several songs, including "To a Skylark" and "Ode to the West Wind", bring out their creators' impeccable sense of rhythm and music. Of all the Romantics, Shelley alone was gifted with the unique power of combining the external rhythm of the verse with the inner rhythm of thought and imagery. Hence Swinburne called him a 'perfect singing god' and followed him with great fidelity when he came to compose his own verses. Swinburne's "Atlanta in Calydon" and "England: An Ode" are the musical lyrics of the first order. Lord Tennyson, among the Victorians, toed the line of Shelley in many of his poems, such as in "The Lady of Shalott", "The Splendour Falls" and "Break, Break, Break".

While discussing 'auditory imagination', our attention is naturally directed towards S.T. Coleridge and his threadbare analysis of the role of 'imagination'. First, Coleridge made subtle distinction between 'fancy' and 'imagination', and then he adroitly bifurcated the functions of 'imagination' into 'primary imagination' and 'secondary imagination'.[22] Coleridge pointed out that 'fancy' attempts to combine things into a shape while 'imagination' fuses them into a harmonious whole. The role of 'fancy' (as seen in the Neo-Classical poets like Dryden and Pope) is merely combinatory, while that of 'imagination' (as found in the Romantics) is creative. The object of 'primary imagination' is to perceive sense-impressions of persons, places, and things—in their parts as well as wholes. The 'secondary imagination' is a composite faculty of the soul, employing all powers of perception, intellect, will, and emotion. It is a more active agent than the primary imagination, and whatever is perceived by the latter it "dissolves, diffuses, dissipates, in order to recreate".[23] Its esemplastic (or unifying) power identifies the mind with nature and nature with the mind, turning the internal into the external and the external into the internal.

Coleridge, however, differs with Wordsworth on the application of poetic diction. Coleridge opines that Wordsworth's statement that poetic diction should be "a selection of the language really spoken by men"[24] is somewhat erroneous and contrary to his own practice in great poems like "Tintern Abbey", "Ode to Immortality" and "The Solitary Reaper". Similarly, Coleridge maintains that Wordsworth's claim that "there neither is, nor can be, any essential difference between the language of prose and metrical composition"[25] is not correct. The use of meter and what Dr. Johnson calls 'flowers of speech' set poetry apart from prose. According to Coleridge, the language of poetry differs from the language of prose in the same way as prose itself differs from the language of conversation.[26] But Wordsworth's view of language is quite similar to that of Eliot in so far as both uphold the sanctity of 'common speech'.

One of the significant critical doctrines of Eliot is the 'unification of sensibility'. This phrase is found in the essay "The Metaphysical Poets" (1921) in *Selected Essays* (1932). Its opposite phrase, the 'dissociation of sensibility', also occurs in that very essay. In evolving these two phrases, Eliot is preoccupied with the question of 'sensibility' for poetic purpose. 'Sensibility' is a term denoting 'the union of thought and feeling' in appropriate proportions. When a poet is able to transform his thought into feeling, we get good poetry, but when he fails to do so we have bad poetry. Eliot particularly mentions Chapman and Donne as the two writers who have "a direct sensuous apprehension of thought" or "a creation of thought into feeling."[27] This kind of admiration is, however, denied to Tennyson and Browning because they "are poets, and they think; but they do not feel their thoughts as immediately as the odour of a rose."[28] Eliot does not spare even Milton and Dryden for the same reason, and yet he praises one or two passages in Shelley's "Triumph of Life" and Keats's "Second Hyperion". In the case of Shelley and Keats (with reference to the above-cited poems), a reader comes across "traces of a struggle toward unification of sensibility."[29]

In his Preface to the second edition of the *Lyrical Ballads*, Wordsworth had stated that "Poems to which any value can be attached" were produced by "a man...possessed of more than usual organic sensibility" who had "thought long and deeply."[30] Coleridge also upheld the same viewpoint in suggesting that no man could ever be "a great poet" without being simultaneously "a profound philosopher."[31] What a poet felt in moments of inspiration was 'modified and directed' by his long and deep thought. Hence, mere 'inspiration' or 'spontaneity' is not enough; what is more needed is the "depth and energy of thought."[32] The function of poetry is not just to please but to elevate a reader, and any elevation is possible only through "the union of deep feeling with profound thought".

Another critical issue of importance is the 'social function of poetry'. This is a point shared by both Eliot and Shelley. Eliot's social criticism is contained in such works as *After Strange Gods* (1934), *The Idea of a Christian Society* (1939), and *Notes toward the Definition of Culture* (1948), and expressed in them his considered views of culture and society. To Eliot, 'culture' signifies 'European culture' and 'society' implies 'western society'. He was against any bloody coups or violent revolutions because they disrupted the healthy growth of culture and created chaos in society. Eliot believed that culture was something complex yet resourceful, and that it was not developed by 'the selected few' or by 'a single source'. Commenting on Eliot's idea of society and culture, Bantock has observed as follows:

> Society, indeed, can only be meaningfully and fruitfully understood by those who start from a proper appreciation of the individual human dilemma, not by those who ignore the paradoxes of life in favour of some abstract and unrealistic belief in the possibility of total harmony and adjustment.... Eliot believed, of course, that society could be organised on better or worse lines....[33]

Eliot's attitude towards society and culture remains largely that of a humanist striving ceaselessly for a better world-order in a tension-ridden age.

Shelley, like Eliot, assigned an explicitly 'social function' to poetry in his *A Defence of Poetry* (1821). Yet, Eliot directed his ire against Shelley in *The Use of Poetry and the Use of Criticism* (1933) and *On Poetry and Poets* (1957). The main accusation of Eliot against Shelley was that the latter's ideas were 'the ideas of adolescence' though both held identical views about the unconscious organic power of poetry, about the employment of images and symbols, and about the mythmaking. Like Eliot, Shelley also felt that there was an intimate connection between poetry and social order. Shelley was undoubtedly a great social reformist and a visionary prophet. He envisioned a happy and healthy society based on his ideas of reform in society. Like a true prophet, he said in his poem "Ode to the West Wind":

> O, Wind,
> If Winter comes, can Spring be far behind?[34]

Shelley's ideas and visions, at times unorthodox and revolutionary, made him a rebel in life. He found fault with all the established institutions and conventions, including the Church and the State. He was actually a socialist at heart, born before his time. Eliot blamed Shelley's *guru*, Godwin, for corrupting the young man's mind and rendering it chaotic and undisciplined. Eliot never tolerated any kind of indiscipline, lawlessness and intellectual incoherence in art. Shelley being an avowed 'atheist' could not stir sympathetic chords within Eliot. Moreover, Shelley advocated the idea of 'free love' and this was an ideological challenge to a man who had declared himself to be a 'conservative' in politics and a 'classicist' in literature. So, the two poets fell part despite the fact that they had identical views on the 'social function' of poetry.

Notes

1. One should look up the early poems of T.S. Eliot contained in *Poems Written in Early Youth*, ed. Valerie Fletcher Eliot (London: Faber & Faber, 1967), for a corroboration of this statement.
2. Cited from Grover Smith, *T.S. Eliot's Poetry and Plays: A Study in Sources and Meaning*, Phenix Books ed., 6th imprint. (Chicago & London: The University of Chicago Press, 1965), p. 304, note 12.
3. T.S. Eliot, "The Function of Criticism", *Selected Essays* (1932; London: Faber & Faber, 1951), p. 25.
4. "Preface", *For Lancelot Andrewes* (London: Faber & Faber, 1928), p. 7.
5. "Tradition and the Individual Talent", *The Sacred Wood* (1920: London: Faber & Faber, 1960), p. 16.
6. *Ibid*., p. 18.
7. *Ibid*., p. 14.
8. *Ibid*., p. 17.
9. William Wordsworth, "Preface to *Lyrical Ballads*", cited from S.T. Coleridge, *Biographia Literaria*, ed. George Sampson (Cambridge: At the University Press, 1920), p. 197.—See also p. 186 for Wordsworth's definition of poetry.
10. William Wordsworth, "Laodamia" *The Poems of William Wordsworth*, Vol. I, ed. Nowell Charles Smith (London: Methuen & Co., 1908), p. 355.
11. T.S. Eliot, "Tradition...", *The Sacred Wood*, p. 21.
12. S.T. Coleridge, *Biographia Literaria*, Vol. II, ed. J. Shawcross (Oxford: At the Clarendon Press, 1907), p. 16.
13. T.S. Eliot, "Hamlet and His Problems", *The Sacred Wood*, p. 100.
14. Douglas Bush, *Mythology and the Romantic Tradition in English Poetry* (New York: Pageant Book Co., 1957), p. 112.
15. John Keats, "Ode to a Nightingale", *Fifteen Poets,* Indian rpt. 7th imprint. (Calcutta: Oxford University Press, 1985), p. 360.
16. Graham Hough, *The Romantic Poets* (London: Hutchinson University Library, 1953), p. 179.

17. Helen Gardner, *The Art of T.S. Eliot* (London: Cresset Press, 1949), pp. 4-5.
18. T.S. Eliot, *The Use of Poetry and the Use of Criticism* (London: Faber & Faber, 1933), p. 118.
19. *Ibid.*, pp. 118-19.
20. T.S. Eliot, "The Music of Poetry", *Selected Prose of T.S. Eliot*, ed. Frank Kermode (1975), p. 112.
21. Coleridge, *Biographia Literaria*, II ed. Shawcross, p. 14.
22. *Ibid.*, I, ed. Shawcross, p. 202.
23. *Idem.*
24. Wordsworth, "Preface to *Lyrical Ballads*", *op. cit.*, p. 189. See Coleridge's *Biographia Literaria,* II, ed. Shawcross, pp. 29-30, for his views.
25. Wordsworth, "Preface to *Lyrical Ballads*", *op. cit.*, p. 189. For Coleridge's opinion on this subject, please look up his *Biographia Literaria*, II (Chapter XVIII), pp. 45-48.
26. Coleridge, *Biographia Literaria*, II (Chapter XVIII), pp. 45 & 62.
27. T.S. Eliot, "The Metaphysical Poets," *Selected Essays*, p. 286.
28. *Ibid.*, p. 287.
29. *Ibid.*, p. 288.
30. Wordsworth, "Preface....", *op. cit.*, p. 186.
31. Coleridge, *Biographia Literaria,* II (Chapter XV), p. 19.
32. *Idem.*
33. G.N. Bantock, *T.S. Eliot and Education* (London: Faber & Faber, 1970), p. 43.
34. P.B. Shelley, "Ode to the West Wind", *Fifteen Poets*, p. 341.

5

Native Modernity in Indian English Fiction*

Modernity is an open-ended term with a wide range of speculation and signification. For one thing, we have to be certain about its specific time of origin. Geoffrey Chaucer belongs to the fourteenth century, but he is called 'the first great modern poet'. G.H. Mair titles his book of literary history *Modern English Literature* (1911) and traces the history of this literature since the fifteenth century. Maybe, he had the Renaissance in his mind—the Renaissance that opened up new vistas and initiated fresh explorations in the areas of arts and literature, science and navigation. But in reality, the wave of modernity swept the shores of Europe, including England, in the first quarter of the twentieth century when a number of literary works of far-reaching significance appeared and shook the very foundation of conventional mode of living and thinking. Of such works, we may mention Joseph Conrad's *Heart of Darkness* (1902), James Joyce's *Ulysses* (1922), and T.S. Eliot's *The Waste Land* (1922), and these works ushered in the age of Modernism in English literature.

Modernity or Modernism largely signifies a drastic change in our traditional attitude and mental setup. Allan Bold in his article "Modernism in Modern Life" contrasts it to 'tradition' and observes that 'tradition' is "entirely different from the

---

* Keynote: Address at the National Seminar held at Dr. Bhagavat Sahai Government P.G. College, Gwalior (M.P.) on 16th March, 2013.

tradition of experimental art that modernism springs from."[1] J.A. Cuddon defines 'modernism' as "a breaking away from established rules, traditions and conventions, fresh ways of looking at man's position and function in the universe and many (in some cases remarkable) experiments in form and style. It is particularly concerned with language and how to use it...."[2] The noted English poet, William Blake (1757-1827), drew a subtle distinction between 'innocence' (traditional sense of virtue) and 'experience' (or 'lost innocence'). Echoing him, Umberto Eco remarks that "modernity is like a man who loves a sophisticated lady very much and knows that he cannot say to her 'I love you madly' because he knows that she knows (and she knows that he knows)...he will nevertheless have said what he wanted to say to the woman that he loves her in an age of lost innocence."[3] In the world of love and romance, modernity is marked by the loss of innocence. T.S. Eliot (1888-1965) in his famous essay "The Metaphysical Poets" points out that variety and complexity are the hallmarks of our civilization[4], which is also modern civilization. The well-known critic, Cleanth Brooks, in his book, *Modern Poetry and the Tradition* (1939), states that modern poetry is 'anti-traditional' and opposed to "lifeless conventions"[5], and this statement is exactly applicable to modern fiction too.

The present essay/paper is devoted to a minute discussion of "Native Modernity in Indian English Fiction". The qualifying word 'native' is somewhat intriguing and seems to suggest that modernity, in the Indian context, has its own brand, its own peculiar traits, its own range and scope, maybe like 'native tradition', 'native customs', 'native dreams', 'native images', 'native feminism', etc. In this connection, we are reminded of the emphatic assertion of Sir Walter Scott: "This is my own, my native land". So 'nativity' adds variety and complexity to a literary convention and movement on the one hand, and functions as a means or mode of connectivity to a global phenomenon. What I suggest here is that modernity/modernism is a global phenomenon, to which Indian modernity/modernism is connected in more than one way.

The focal point of this essay/paper is Indian English Fiction *vis-à-vis* Modernity. I have chosen merely a few novelists and their texts as samples of native modernity for my discussion here. They are picked up as models of innovation and experiment in the areas of theme, technique and language. Raja Rao from among "the Big Three",[6] Arun Joshi, Anita Desai, Shashi Deshpande, Arundhati Roy and Aravind Adiga are some of the notable modernists whose one or two texts will be examined here to show how they try to break a new ground, away from the conventional and beaten track, in their respective works.

As regards Raja Rao, he stands apart from Mulk Raj Anand and R.K. Narayan in the handling of language and narrative technique. His fictional language does not display any propensity for colloquial idioms or abusive phrases as Mulk Raj Anand usually does in his novels, nor for the chaste yet crystal-clear academic vocabulary that R.K. Narayan uses in his writings. Raja Rao's language has a remarkable flow and breathless rush in "the repeated use of inverted syntax" in his *Kanthapura* (1938), where "the sentences chase one another", according to Prof. M.K. Naik, "with adjective crowding adjective and the 'toe' of one noun touching 'the heel' of another...."[7] This kind of structure creates a lyrical prose, and *Kanthapura* comes out as a masterpiece of word-painting. As a result, his descriptions of certain scenes and events assume extra charm. There is a sort of lyrical fluency and hurried rush in his descriptions and narrations; for example, in describing the coming of the first rain he writes:

> It churns and splashes, beats against the treetops, reckless and wilful, and suddenly floating forwards, it bucks back and spits forward and pours down upon the green, weak coffee leaves, thumbing down to the earth, and then playfully longing up, the coffee leaves rising with it, and whorling and winnowing, spurting and rattling, it jerks and snorts this side and that.[8]

Raja Rao's language becomes simply lyrical in the face of natural beauty, reminding us of John Keats in its concreteness and sensuousness. His use of evocative and innovative similes enhances the overall effect of his narratives. For instance, after the first fury of the rain the darkness descends upon the village and "grows thick as sugar in a cauldron" and the thunder "goes dashing like a temple cymbal".

Raja Rao's narrative skill has been praised by scholars like C.D. Narasimhaiah and M.K. Naik, though he admits that—

> The telling has not been easy. One has to convey in a language that is not one's own and the spirit that is one's own.... Yet English is not really an alien language to us. It is the language of our intellectual make-up—like Sanskrit or Persian was before—but not of our emotional make-up. We are all instinctively bilingual, many of us writing in our own language and in English. We cannot write like the English. We should not.[9]

Raja Rao is credited to have Indianized English. His narrative technique comes close to the Puranic technique, and he infuses in his narratives "a greater facility for capturing the variety of Sanskrit rhythms and modes of expression".[10] In writing *The Serpent and the Rope* (1960), a most ambitious work indeed, Raja Rao is indebted to both French and Sanskrit. He goes to the French language for "discipline and grace",[11] for "temptation to elegance—to rhetoric",[12] and for "both the 'dexterity in the manipulation' and 'temptation to rhetoric'",[13] and to Sanskrit for its "range of varied expression, suppleness, and adaptability to different modes and effects, and similar richness and complexity."[14] Raja Rao's technique clearly carries the effect of the *puranas*, the story within story. It raises the narrative to a spiritual or metaphysical plane. That's why Ramaswamy, the protagonist of *The Serpent and the Rope*, says that "He who possesses Sanskrit can possess himself".[15]

If Raja Rao raises the fiction to the spiritual-cum-philosophical level, quite in tune with our native custom and culture, Arun Joshi lifts it to the psychological level. Joshi's inner explorations resemble those of Anita Desai in her fiction. His five novels are full of struggle, tension and conflicts. *The Strange Case of Billy Biswas* (1971), which is more powerful than *The Last Labyrinth* (1981) or *The City and The River* (1989), may be taken up as a model of case study, where the protagonist is portrayed as "a psychic person given to conscience and sometimes to visions and hallucinations."[16] He is a Ph.D. in Anthropology from the University of New York. On returning to India, he gets married to a 'mod', Meena Chatterjee, whose only concern in life is to make money. A son is born to them. In the meantime, Biswas has become a teacher in the University of Delhi. But getting much and more restive with the lifestyle of a big metropolitan city, he disappears in the jungles of Madhya Pradesh. Away from the so-called civilized world, he falls in love with a tribal woman called Bilasia. During one of the visits of the collector to villages, his wife Situ becomes seriously ill and Biswas is invited to cure her for good. Biswas tells his friend, the Collector, that any attempts to trace him will prove disastrous to him. Situ informs Biswas's wife Meena and his father about his whereabouts. At the request of his wife and father, the Chief Secretary at Bhopal intervenes in the matter and a police party is sent out to capture him but in vain, Biswas ultimately dies of bullet injuries. The novel powerfully highlights the sense of alienation and estrangement of modern man, reminding us of Wordsworth's didactic sonnet "The world is too much with us".

As mentioned above, Anita Desai in her novels—about a dozen—excels in evoking the image of modern restless women, especially in the first phase of her career beginning with *Cry, The Peacock* (1963) through *Where Shall We Go This Summer?* (1971) and *Fire on the Mountain* (1977) to *Clear Light of Day* (1980). Maya in *Cry, The Peacock*, Sita in *Where Shall We Go This Summer?* Nanda Kaul in *Fire on the Mountain* and Bim in *Clear Light of Day* are all troubled souls in one way or the other. They are largely psychic cases to be closely studied by psychiatrists, like Celia in T.S. Eliot's *The Cocktail Party* (1950). But we must remember that the question of survival for women, and survival with dignity, has been a paramount question in our society, and this has been forcefully articulated by Mrs. Desai in her novels. Jasbir Jain may call it "In Pursuit of Wholeness",[17] but this is also a pursuit of loneliness and estrangement in human relations.

As contrasted to the viewpoint of Anita Desai towards womankind is the attitude of Shashi Deshpande in her novels. Obviously, Deshpande does not go to the extent of allowing adultery and extramarital relations in building the image of 'new woman' in her novels, as Nayantara Sahgal and Shobha De would do, but she does depict a realistic picture of man-woman relationship in them. Saru or Sarita, the protagonist of *The Dark Holds No Terrors* (1980), becomes a doctor of repute and a better earning member of the family, and this breeds a sense of inferiority in her husband of meagre means who turns a sadist in nocturnal meetings with her. In her utter helplessness, she goes away to her Baba who advises her to be with Manu, her husband. Where is the solution to her personal problems? A similar situation obtains in *That Long Silence* (1988), where Jaya and Mohan develop an estranged relationship, so much so that they are not even on talking terms. At last, it is Jaya who decides to break the ice of silence, true to the native custom and culture. Thus, Deshpande treads the middle path as a feminist (if she is one at all), not the aggressive path of the Western feminists. This is what prompts Mukta Arey and Viney Kirpal to remark in their perceptive study of Shashi Deshpande as follows: "So what makes Indian women 'feminists' different is the fact that they raise their voice against social injustice and oppression of woman rather than ask for her freedom from the institution of marriage and family."[18]

Shashi Deshpande's treatment of womankind is undeniably modernist, and so is Arundhati Roy in her theme and form, and in her language and style. Roy's *The God of Small Things* (1997) picks up a burning social issue—that of rigid caste system—in which Ammukutty, a divorcee with two children belonging to an upper stratum of society, falls in love with an educated young man named Velutha of a lower class. Ammu is a great daydreamer who ever dreams of "one-armed man".[19] She starts meeting this young man in a haunted house across the river Meenachal. Her aunt, Baby Kochamma, lodges a report with the police that Velutha, a parvan (an untouchable), has forced himself upon Ammu and on the basis of this false report Velutha is arrested, beaten badly with boots and batons, and thrown bleeding into the lock-up where he dies in midnight. The tragic incident gives great shock to Ammu who also breathes her last subsequently. At that time, she is simply "thirty-one. Not old, not young, but a viable-die-able age."[20] Thus, the tyrannical society has taken away the lives of two loving souls.

Apart from the subject-matter, Arundhati Roy's language and style are highly spicy and innovative. She skillfully coins new and compound words, such as "Thiswayandthat" (p. 101), "Stoppited" (p. 141), "Locusts Stand I" (p. 57), and "Myooozick" (p. 95). Frequently she takes liberty with the use of punctuation marks and capital letters, for example.

> She used her windows for specific purposes.
> For a Breath of Fresh Air.
> To Pay for the Milk. To Let Out a Trapped Wasp. (p. 28)

At times her language becomes highly imagistic and arresting. For example,

> History's smell.
> Like old roses on a breeze. (p. 55)

And again:

> When the gurgling, bubbling sound came, she [Baby Kochamma] listened with her eyes. A yellow brook burbled through a mountain pass. (p. 95)

This latter passage presents a graphic picture of a fatty woman urinating and watching the 'yellow water' jetting forth. It is free from inhibitions and tends to be modernistic in details. It recalls T.S. Eliot's modernistic image in the following lines of "The Love Song of J. Alfred Prufrock":

> Let us go then, you and I,
> When the evening is spread out against the sky
> Like a patient etherised upon the table.[21]

Arundhati Roy tries to demolish the age-old caste system when she remarks about Inspector Thomas Mathew that he has "a Touchable wife, two Touchable daughters—whole Touchable generations waiting in their Touchable wombs..." (p. 259). This Inspector keeps tapping Ammu's breasts with his baton as though he is "choosing mangoes from a basket" (p. 8). Thus, Mrs. Roy is highly modernistic in her theme, language and style.

Aravind Adiga is also remarkably modernist in his content and form in the novel *The White Tiger* (2008). It is an autobiographical novel cast in the epistolary form. It begins as a letter addressed to the Chinese Premier, Mr. Wen Jiabao, stationed in Beijing, the capital of China. The letter is written by 'the White Tiger' from Bengaluru (India), a centre of technology and outsourcing. We have to remember that the growth of science and technology, of logic and enlightenment, is a valuable part of modernity. Here in this novel, the narrator Balram Halwai recounts his own story of rising from the position of a poor man, being the son of a rickshaw-puller born in the village called Laxmangarh in the district of Gaya (Bihar) where Lord Buddha sat under a leafy *peepal* tree and found his enlightenment, to the position of a very prosperous businessman. Very fast he develops from a driver of Mr. Ashok, the son of the village landlord called the Stork presently settled in Dhanbad, whom he kills mercilessly in Delhi and runs away with his red bag of money—"seven hundred thousand rupees"[22]—to Bangalore along with his cousin, to be a big businessman; in other words, he rises from "a social entrepreneur to a business entrepreneur".[23] At the close of the novel, Balram lays out a chart for his own future. He says, "I'm thinking of real estate next" (p. 319). And after remaining three or four years in real estate, he will sell everything, take the money, and start a school—an English language school—for poor children in Bengaluru. It will be a school full of White Tigers, unleashed on the city of Bengaluru.

To conclude, the above discussion shows clearly that there are many talented writers who have moved away from "the old, unhappy, far-off things/ And battles long ago", as Wordsworth puts it in his poem "The Solitary Reaper", and broken new grounds in Indian English Fiction. Raja Rao, Arun Joshi, Anita Desai, Shashi Deshpande, Arundhati Roy and Aravind Adiga are some such talented writers. This list may be further lengthened by incorporating the names of Mulk Raj Anand, R.K. Narayan, G.V. Desani, Kamala Markandaya, Manohar Malgonkar, Bhabani Bhattacharya, V.S. Naipaul, Salman Rushdie, and Manju Kapur. They all are imaginatively fertile and thematically and linguistically modernist. A study of these or at least some of these Indian English fictionists in the light of their modernity/ modernism will prove highly rewarding to readers and researchers in English.

Notes

1. Allan Bold, "Modernism in Modern Life," *Twentieth-Century Poetry* (Walton Hall, Milton Keynes: The Open University Press, 1975), p. 228.
2. J.A. Cuddon, "Modernism", *The Penguin Dictionary of Literary Terms and Literary Theory* (Harmondsworth & London: Penguin Books, 1999 ed.), pp. 515-16.
3. Umberto Eco on "Modernity"; cited from N. Krishnaswamy, John Varghese & Sunita Mishra, *Contemporary Literary Theory: A Student's Companion* (New Delhi: Macmillan Publishers India Ltd., 2001), pp. 25-26.
4. T.S. Eliot, "The Metaphysical Poets", *Selected Essays* (London: Faber & Faber, 1932), p. 289.
5. Cleanth Brooks, "The Modern Poet and the Tradition", *Modern Poetry and the Tradition*, A Galaxy Bool ed. (1939; New York: Oxford University Press, 1965), p. 69.
6. William Walsh has used the phrase "the Big Three" for Mulk Raj Anand, R.K. Narayan and Raja Rao. See his article in *Indian Writing in English*, ed. Ramesh Mohan (Madras: Orient Longman Ltd., 1973), pp. 26-36.
7. M.K. Naik, "Coils of the Serpent: Raja Rao and the 'Unreal' World", *Studies in Contemporary Indian Fiction in English*, ed. A.N. Dwivedi (Allahabad: Kitab Mahal, 1987), pp. 163-64.
8. Raja Rao, *Kanthapura* (Madras Oxford University Press, 1974), p. 73.
9. Raja Rao, "Author's Foreword", *Kanthapura*, p. v.
10. Narsingh Srivastava, "The Narrative Technique of Raja Rao", *Studies in Contemporary Indian Fiction in English*, ed. A.N. Dwivedi, p. 177.
11. A.P. O'Brien, "A Meeting with Raja Rao", *Prajna* (B.H.U. Journal), XI, No. 2 (1966), clxxxiii.
12. André Gide, "*The Ethics of the Artist* (London: 1950), p. 3; cited from M.K. Naik, *Raja Rao* (Boston: Twayne Publishers Inc., 1972), p. 35.
13. M.K. Naik, *Raja Rao*, p. 35.
14. *Ibid.*, pp. 26-27.
15. Raja Rao, *The Serpent and the Rope* (1960; Delhi: Hind Pocket Books, 1968), p. 35.

16. A.N. Dwivedi, "The Novels of Arun Joshi: A Critical Study", *Studies in Contemporary Indian Fiction in English* (1987), p. 310.
17. Jasbir Jain, "In Pursuit of Wholeness: Transcendence of the Self in the Novels of Anita Desai", *Studies in Contemporary Indian Fiction in English*, ed. A.N. Dwivedi (1987), pp. 298-308.
18. Mukta Atrey and Viney Kirpal, "Introduction", *Shashi Deshpande: A Feminist Study of Her Fiction* (Delhi: B.R. Publishing Corporation, 1988), pp. 5-6.
19. Who is this "one-armed man"? The novelist suggests that he is:

    The God of Loss.

    The God of Small Things.

    The God of Goose Bumps and Sudden Smiles.

    —*The God of Small Things* (New Delhi: IndiaInk Publishing Co. Pvt. Ltd., 1997), p. 330.
20. *Ibid.*, p. 161.

    The subsequent references to this novel are given in the body of the paper itself.
21. T.S. Eliot, *Collected Poems* (London: Faber & Faber, 1963), p. 13.
22. Aravind Adiga, *The White Tiger* (Noida, U.P.: Harper Collins Publishers, 2008), p. 281.
23. *Ibid.*, p. 299.

    The subsequent references to this novel are given in the body of the paper itself.

6

Postmodernism in Indian English Fiction: Issues and Challenges

Postmodernism emerged as a movement first in architecture then in other disciplines such as literature, visual art (especially photography), music, dance, film and theatre, in the 1970s, with the publication of Jean-Francois Lyotard's *La Condition Postmoderne* (1978; English version, 1984) and Jean Baudrillard's *Simulations* (1981; English translation 1983). In his perceptive book, *The Postmodern Condition* (English version), Lyotard raises his objections, and targets at, to the contemporary German theorist Jurgen Habermas's postulations that a major moment in the history of 'postmodernism' is the rise of the Enlightenment or the so-called the Age of Reason (Peter Barry: 2007, 85; Linda Hutcheon: 2006, 115). Habermas in his bright paper, "Modernity an Incomplete Project," strives to see 'postmodernism' as an extension/continuation of 'modernism' which in turn is the culmination of the salient features of the Enlightenment (the period of one hundred years from the mid-seventeenth to the mid-eighteenth century), with its insistence on reason, purpose, coherence and order. Niall Lucy in his book, *Postmodern Literary Theory* (in Chapter 12) pleads for 'the Return of Reason' in the postmodern age (1997; 2002, 247-49). The cultural or literary movement called 'modernism', in the view of Peter Barry, constituted "a lament for a lost sense of purpose, a lost coherence, a lost system of values" (2007, 85). Against the backdrop of such a sense of modernism and loss of values (as we may come across in T.S. Eliot's *The Waste Land*,

1922), postmodernism came into existence. Linda Hutcheon aptly points out that postmodernism appears before us in various shades and colours: "For some it was a mere 'moment', while for others it was a more general 'condition'. Some denigrated it to just a 'style'; still others elevated it to a historical period" (2006, 115). Here, in this paper, we will examine postmodernism in its diverse shades and variations, taking into account its dominant issues and challenges and illustrating them, wherever possible, from Indian English Fiction of our times.

I

What is Postmodernism?

Defining 'postmodernism' is in itself a challenging task, for, as hinted above, it carries with it multiple shades and interpretations. However, it may be taken as a derivation from 'modernism', a movement in architecture, art and literature that marked an extension/a continuation of 'modernism' as well as a discounting of modernist tendencies. Linda Hutcheon hints at this truth when she states that "the very word 'postmodern' illustrates this [that it incorporates within itself the deconstructable traces of its own contradictions], for it carries within itself the 'modern' from which it both derives and deviates. It is 'post' in the sense of both temporally 'after' and conceptually 'beyond' (2006, 117). As we know, in the temporal sense, 'modernism' flourished in the first half of the twentieth century, and since the 1960s a marked shift in the taste/attitude of artists and writers was perceptible and 'postmodernism' became an in-thing in the last two decades of the twentieth century and the early twenty-first century. In contemporary Indian English Fiction, postmodernism made its inroads with the publication of Salman Rushdie's *Midnight's Children* in 1981.

Jacques Derrida, a poststructuralist thinker who derived much from Saussure in his consideration of 'language', discounted the relationship between language and the visible world (*i.e.* nature) and discovered 'the metaphysics of presence' to be false. He thought that the relationship of language to reality (or nature) is not definable or reliable, because all language systems are 'inherently unreliable cultural constructs'. While considering 'the question of agency' that ushered in 'the postcolonial and the postmodern', Derrida held the view that "[F] or some of us the principle of indeterminism is what makes the conscious freedom of man fathomable" (My chances/Mes chances, cited from Homi K. Bhabha: 1994, 245). In Derrida's opinion, then, 'the principle of indeterminism' is the guiding principle of postmodernism (as well as of postcolonialism, as the two are interrelated in many respects). And this principle works to unite postcolonialism and postmodernism at a certain point. The forces of postcolonialism and postmodernism combined with those of poststructuralism, feminism and subalternism have generated an unprecedented atmosphere of challenging the established authority, law and order in society, even the traditionally recognised borders of nation-state (such as we witness in the 1980s and onwards), so that dynamic avant-gardism was born in artistic and socio-political spheres. Consequently, as Homi Bhaba puts it, the figure of man gets 'de-historicized' and dislodged: "The invisible power that is invested in this 'de-historicized' figure of man is gained at the cost of those 'others'—women, natives, the colonized, the indentured and enslaved who, at the same time but in other spaces, were becoming the peoples without a history" (1994, 282).

Jean-Francois Lyotard in raising his objections to two 'metanarratives' or 'master narratives'—the progressing role of history in emancipating humanity and the triumph of science—defines 'postmodernism' as "incredulity towards meta-narratives" (cited from Christopher Butler: 2002, 13). Elaborating his viewpoint, Lyotard observes that these metanarratives implied by major philosophies like Kantianism, Hegelianism, and Marxism, which argue that history is constantly progressive and that knowledge (science) can unfailingly liberate us, are in crisis and in decline. Lyotard contends that such doctrines/narratives have 'lost their credibility' since the Second World War.

Situating the Postmodern

Modernism and Postmodernism are ways of looking at things, conditions of the mind and ways of living life. Postmodernism may be called 'the Age of Virtual Reality', not 'the Age of Stark

Reality' as Modernism was during the two Great Wars. The term 'Virtual Reality' may perhaps best be understood when we keep in mind the existence of Virtual University or Virtual Education today through the medium of Distance Education that crosses the boundaries of a university/an institution. Jean Baudrillard appropriately calls it 'simulations of the real'.

It was Ihab Hassan, an American critic, who first tried to establish a link between a certain kind of modernist avant-garde writing and postmodernism in literature. In his famous article, "Toward a Concept of Postmodernism", published in *The Postmodern Turn* (1987), he discovered in James Joyce's experimental novel, *Finnegans Wake* (1939), the early signs of the postmodern. Later on, Hassan became famous for his categorization of modernism and postmodernism in terms of countraries or binary oppositions. In his categorization, modernism stood for form, purpose and hierarchy whereas postmodernism represented anti-form, play and anarchy (Hassan: 1987, 91-92).

Obviously, the 'postmodern' may be best situated by placing it besides the 'modern'. Linda Hutcheon aptly suggests that the postmodern openly deviated from three high modernist tenets—its concentration on form; its belief in the autonomy of the work of art and hence its separation from the social and historical world; its insistence on the firm distinction between high art and consumer or mass culture (2006, 118). But in certain other matters, postmodernism learnt much from modernism and continued the modernist practice, such as the breaking down of the borders between art and life, between the elite and the popular, and the challenging of the existence of any single truth. Also, the ironic parody of James Joyce continued to find its echo in the fiction of American author, Thomas Pynchon, and in that of the controversial British feminist writer Angela Caster. Similarly, works of art or novels containing self-commentary (which may be termed as self-reflexive or metafictional) continued to be written in the postmodernist period too (though the beginning was made in James' *Ulysses*, 1922).

There exists, thus, a complicated relationship between modernism and its 'post'; it may be 'one of critical rethinking'.

In some issues, it is a continuation, and often intensification, of irony, parody, pastiche, and self-reflexivity; in some others, it is a rejection of history, boundaries of nation-state, and barriers of art and life as well as of the elite and the popular. The cultural and artistic relationship between the two is, however, based upon another broader one that is social and political in essence; it has its roots in the works of earlier famous German thinkers, such as Friedrich Nietzsche (a well-known philosopher), Karl Marx (a socio-political thinker) and Sigmund Freud (the founder of psychoanalysis).

Postmodernism: Issues and Challenges

Before initiating a discussion of the main issues and challenges of postmodernism, it would be appropriate to draw a subtle distinction between the two terms—postmodernism and postmodernity. It this context, Linda Hutcheon remarks that "postmodernism is usually used to talk about cultural and artistic dimensions, while postmodernity usually connotes the more general, social and political context" (2006, 119). But generally, the two are not easily separable.

One of the primary issues and challenges of 'postmodernism' is that it has no centre to hold things together. The postmodern world does not follow any principle of centrality or fixity and hence it relies on parody and pastiche which borrow materials/quotes/sentences from other literary and artistic texts. W.B. Yeats, a very perceptive poet indeed, hints at this postmodernist situation when in his famous poem "The Second Coming" he writes thus:

> Things fall part, the centre cannot hold;
> Mere anarchy is loosed upon the world,
> The blood dimmed tide is loosed, and everywhere
> The ceremony of innocence is drowned;
> The best lack all conviction, while the worst
> Are full of passionate intensity.
> (*The Works of W.B. Yeats*, 1994, 158)

Here the poet has become prophetic in predicting the birth of postmodernism from the bowels of modernism. The postmodern condition, about which the French theorists talk so warmly sixty years later, is remarkably depicted by Yeats in the above-quoted poetic passage.

Lack of 'the centre' has overturned the applecart of human life in our time. It has annihilated man's conviction and beliefs and let loose bloodshed and anarchy in the world around. The growth of science, or what we usually call 'scientific reason', has eroded the very base of religion and conviction in our day. Matthew Arnold's Sea of Faith is not merely on a decline but also has left us in a welter of uncertainty, in a crisis of indeterminism, in a stage of unending flux. And we are forced to live the life of alarms and confusion, of chaos and disorder, like Arnold's ignorant soldiers fighting in darkness:

> And we are here as on a darkling plain
> Swept with confused alarms of struggle and flight;
> Where ignorant armies clash by night.
> ("Dover Beach": 1954; 1967, 64)

The present-day living condition has become so dismal and chaotic because of an unprecedented triumph of science and technology. We are now living in the cyber age, which has thrown us into a state of uncertainty, lack of the centre, indeterminism, faithlessness, lack of conviction, and virtual reality.

Christopher Butler, a noted postmodernist scholar, thinks that the postmodernist artists, academic critics, astute philosophers and social scientists may be put together as "members of a loosely constituted and quarrelsome political party", and that this party is "by and large internationalist and progressive" (2002, 2). He further says that this party is "not particularly unified in doctrine" and that it is "certain of its uncertainty" (2002, 2). The postmodernist attitude is, therefore, "one of a suspicion that can border on paranoia" (2002, 3). In promoting a skeptical attitude in art and literature, Lyotard's contribution is substantial; he questions, as suggested earlier, the traditional role of history and the triumph of science (and calls them metanarratives based on false notions). This kind of skeptical attitude can also be discovered in the novels of Salman Rushdie, Arundhati Roy, Kiran Desai and Aravind Adiga.

Postmodernism is also interpreted, as the Marxist critics do, as an ideology that is ideally suited to express and advance the global economic system based on consumerism and capitalism. Fredric Jameson, a distinguished Marxist critic of America, saw in the postmodern, a negative 'cultural logic of late capitalism', while Jean Baudrillard, a noted French sociologist, looked at it as a crisis in representing and understanding the human world around us. The high consumerist capitalism necessarily weans away consumers from traditional/established practices/styles in order to take them to a department store/supermarket/mall where bits and pieces of articles are exhibited in glittering packages (2001, 19). This sort of consumerist capitalism is ceaselessly promoted by mass media, electronic media, sky shops and super-jet transportation. This kind of consumerist culture has cut across the national borders and deprived us of a sense of history. The huge growth of mass media and electronic media has reduced the world to what Marshall McLuhan in the 1960s called the 'electronic village' (or, the 'global village').

Related to this development is the pro-receptive attitude of the postmodern to 'video/TV/Internet fiction' with fragmented images that can be erased, moved forward and backward with the help of latest mechanisms, and operated at a fast speed, as against the old style 'photo fiction' of the past. The postmodern generation prefers short episodes to lengthy narratives and is inclined towards brief but intense living and not towards dull and dry living.

Postmodernism as a way of life, a state of mind, subverts everything that is established, rigid or serious; it frankly questions and mocks such things. It has reduced the length and breadth of the world considerably and turned it, as stated above, into 'a global village', a federation of cultures. Consequently, the world has become a marketplace, a selling centre, a jamboree or a carnival with no fixed rules or privileges for anyone, as Lyotard suggests. Postmodernism, thus, creates a living condition in which man tends to adopt a non-serious and comic tone and attitude. Peter Barry has noted the difference of tone and attitude between modernism and postmodernism, and he suggests that the former "is linked with 'high asceticism' while the latter with 'gaudiness' and 'bad taste' mixtures of qualities" (2007, 84-85).

Another important thing about postmodernism is that it does not promote heroic epics, noble heroes/knights/warriors, and grand narratives that sublimate our thoughts and emotions. It rather trusts in 'self-help' and one's own resources. So, outside help of any kind, including religion or charity, is immaterial. Today, many 'self-help' books are on display at the bookstalls of railway stations and bus-stops. Hence it may be said that postmodernists are ever on the move, and migrancy is one of its acknowledged components. With migrancy come displacement and destabilization. That's why life, especially in metropolitan cities, has become so fast, so intense, so-compassionless today.

Postmodernism, like modernism, gives great prominence to fragmentation as a feature of twentieth century art and culture, but its mood in responding to fragmentation is quite different from that of modernism. Ezra Pound calls his *Cantos* a 'rag-bag', implying thereby that this is all that is possible in the modern age. So is T.S. Eliot's *The Waste Land* (1922), a work wherein the poetic persona says, "These fragments I have shored against my ruins...(C.P.: 1963, 5th imprint. 1970, 79). Salman Rushdie's protagonist in *Midnight's Children* (1981), Saleem Sinai, is a split personality with no definite identity or location. At one point, he becomes a metaphor of India's history, at another he defies historical/national boundaries. He is ever on the move, like Balram Halwai in Aravind Adiga's *The White Tiger* (2008). For the modernists, fragmentation breeds a "deep nostalgia for an earlier age when faith was full and authority intact", but for the postmodernists it is "an exhilarating, liberating phenomenon, symptomatic of our escape from the claustrophobic embrace of fixed systems of belief". In short, the modernist "laments fragmentation while the postmodernist celebrates it" (Barry: 2007, 84). Homi Bhabha remarks that postmodernism, for Jameson, is "a doubly inscribed designation", and that it refers to "the naming of a historical event" and "late multinational capitalism" (1994, 306). Bhabha hastens to add that "Jameson uses the languages of psychoanalysis...to provide a genealogy for the subject of *cultural fragmentation*" (307; italics mine).

And finally, postmodernism does not simply signify a completely new epoch or absolute rupture with the modern era but also an altered state of mind, a new series of social and cultural tendencies and attitudes. Primarily, it signals 'the disappearance of the real' (Baudrillard) and 'the loss of credulity in metanarratives' (Lyotard). It is also prone to the mixing of literary genres (the thriller, the detective story, the myth saga, and the psychological novel, etc.), as Peter Barry suggests. It foregrounds what might be called 'intertextual elements' in literature, such as parody, pastiche, and allusion. It does not believe, as the modernist does, in destroying the past or recalling it with a sense of nostalgia; rather it realizes that the past must be revisited, with a sense of 'irony' (Peter Brooker: 1992, 227). It upholds the principle of lack of the centre, suspicion, anarchy, disorder, and fragmentation (Barry maintains that it exults in fragmentation, 2007, 84). It also foregrounds the element of 'narcissism' in narrative technique, where novels focus on and debate their own ends and processes, and thereby 'de-naturalize' their content. Also, postmodernism challenges the distinction between high and low culture and highlights texts which work as hybrid blends of the two (see Homi Bhabha's theory of 'hybridity' in his critical discourse). And to understand it in a proper perspective, as Ania Loomba puts it, there is a need "to distinguish between thinkers who adopt postmodernism as a philosophical creed, and others who signal the need for new tools to understand the contemporary world" (1998; 2001, 251).

II

In this section, I will briefly examine only three fictional works as samples of postmodernist texts, and these works are: Salman Rushdie's *Midnight's Children* (1981), Arundhati Roy's *The God of Small Things* (1997)and Aravind Adiga's *The White Tiger* (2008). Of course, I am aware of the fact that there are some other novels which clearly contain the postmodernist strands, but the three novels chosen for my study here are enough to show how far they go to meet the postmodernist paradigms.

Rushdie's *Midnight's Children* has fetched for him the prestigious Man Booker Prize in 1981 and then the Booker of Bookers' Prize in 1993 and has proved to be a trend-setter in

Indian English Fiction, nay in English Fiction as a whole. This novel is a postmodernist text with its irreverent treatment of historical, political and religious themes and its magical realist style of writing, reminding us of his other novels like *Shame* (1983), *The Satanic Verses* (1988), *The Moor's Last Sigh* (1995), and *The Enchantress of Florence* (2008). Rushdie has garnered much notoriety since the pronouncement of death-sentence on him by Iran's erstwhile President Ayatollah Khomeini for his blasphemous representation of the *Quran* and the Prophet Muhammad in his novel *The Satanic Verses*.

Midnight's Children is a postmodernist novel dealing with the life-story of Saleem Sinai (who narrates the story in the first person). In fact, Saleem's story is simultaneously a story of India's independence and hence it has been described as a national allegory. Saleem's birth was celebrated by the Indian Prime Minister, Pt. Jawaharlal Nehru, and by newspapers such as *The Times of India* and many others, and this prompts Saleem to imagine himself as a figure of national importance. As the novel opens, hints are thrown that historical events will be important in the overall structure of the novel and that Saleem's growth will be inextricably linked to the growth of India. Saleem says:

> I was born in the city of Bombay...once upon a time. No, that won't do, there's no getting away from the date: I was born in Doctor Narlikar's Nursing Home on August 15th, 1947. And the time: the time matters, too. Well then: at night. No, it's important to be more.... On the stroke of midnight, as a matter of fact. Clock hands joined palms in respectful greeting as I came. Oh, spell it out, spell it out: at the precise instant of India's arrival at independence, I tumbled forth into the world.... I had been mysteriously handcuffed to history, my destinies indissolubly chained to those of my country. For the next three decades, there was to be no escape.... And there are so many stories to tell, too many such an excess of intertwined lives events miracles places rumours, so dense a commingling of the improbable and the mundane. (*Midnight's Children*: 1981; 1995, 2)

As a postmodernist text, history is presented here in a fragmented shape-one vast subcontinent is broken into two free nations. It is a kind of dehistoricization of history, a kind of its fragmentation, and a kind of its disfiguration. In this novel, the boundaries of nation-state are in a flux, are deconstructed and then reconstructed. Time and space do not hold ground. Also, personal history is merged into national history and *vice versa*. Stephen Morton rightly remarks in his book, *Salman Rushdie: Fictions of Postcolonial Modernity* (2008), that events in Saleem's own family life "influence and even cause events of national significance, such as the Amritsar massacre, the riots over language, India's independence and subsequent partition and the Indo-Pakistan war of 1965" (36).

Saleem's claim that he belongs to the elite family of Aadam Aziz, his grandfather, who was a medical doctor born in Kashmir, turns out to be false and imaginary. At the end of the novel, Saleem discovers that he is the bastard offspring of William Methwold, a British colonial landowner, and Vanita, one of Methwold's maidservants. Thus, he is an illegitimate child of a British landowner and a subaltern. Certainly, he is an Anglo-Indian—'An Anglo', as Padma puts it in short (*M.C.*: 1981; 1995, 118). His position of 'hybridity' forces him into a position of economic and social marginalization in India. True to his genealogy, Saleem establishes his relationship with the socially and economically backward or subaltern characters, such as Tai, Mary Pereira, Joseph D'Costa, Padma, Parvati, Picture Singh and Shiva. Some scholars like Neil ten Kortenaar (2004, 29-47) and Stephen Morton (2008, 37-39) do not find "the representation of the subaltern" satisfactory and sufficient in *Midnight's Children*.

Apart from the distorted/allegorical treatment of history to be found in *Midnight's Children*, we come across "so many stories" in it, "too many such as excess of intertwined lives events miracles places rumours..." (2). Thus, the novel meets the requirement of Lyotard that metanarratives are not to be had in postmodernist texts, and that small episodes/events are linked together in them in a somewhat loose chain. Besides Saleem's story, there are the stories of his grandfather, father, Padma (the beloved of Saleem), Tai, midnight's children, etc., in the texture of *Midnight's Children*.

One special postmodernist feature of this novel is that it makes use of the magical realism technique in a conspicuous manner, a technique in which Rushdie is a past master. The narrator of the story, Saleem Sinai, is born with a thousand other children at the stroke of midnight on 15th August 1947, all gifted with telepathic powers and abnormal traits. There is a child who can travel through time and another who can change sex at will. Saleem's magical power enabled him to tour through India and to whore all over Karachi; it enabled him to spy on his mother and aunt. His telepathy was responsible for depriving him of the reader's sympathy as he betrayed Sheikh Mujibur Rehman of Bangladesh to the Pakistani enemy as well as the other midnight's children to their murderers. By spying on his mother Amina Sinai, he could know about her secret meetings with her previous husband Nadir Khan (a notorious man), at the Pioneer Cafe (216). Moreover, Saleem had a mini telescope fitted in his large nose which supplied him with all the necessary information about those others who were born at midnight. Besides, Saleem's *ayah* (nurse) called Mary Pereira and the boatman Tai also contribute their shares to further the magical realism technique. The *ayah* talks of supernatural events occurring in the streets of Bombay and of magical events picked up from the *Bible* (304). The old man Tai narrates some oral tales, connecting thereby the oral tradition with the written one.

Such a novel as *Midnight's Children* cast in the magic realist technique and consisting of a series of episodes/events can't claim to have the centrality of plot-structure and theme. And this renders the novel a typically postmodernist text.

The technique of magic (al) realism is also used by Rushdie in his novel *The Enchantress of Florence,* which unfolds a chain of dreams and omens, beliefs in magic and sorcery, and occasionally even the visions of the dead. In *The Enchantress...,* the narrative is woven around a European traveller called Mogor dell' Amore (*i.e.*, the Mughal of Love) arriving at the royal court of Akbar and claiming to be the child of one Qara Koz (*i.e.*, Lady Black Eyes), who deeply loved Argalia, a very brave Florentine soldier.

The European traveller does not disclose his identity unto the very last.

Another postmodernist novel dealing with India's social and political history, its rigid caste structures, its gender bias is *The God of Small Things* (1997) by Arundhati Roy. Hans Bertens, the well-known writer of *The Idea of the Post-modern* (1995), comments in his book, *Literary Theory: The Basics* (2001), that "it [postmodernist writing] unsettles and deconstructs traditional notions about language, about identity, about writing itself, and so on" (141). In Arundhati Roy's novel under review, we come across a good deal of experimentation about language and identity as well as a new dimension of feminism (which is also an offshoot of postmodernism, just as poststructuralism and postcolonialism are the other cognate disciplines/spheres). So, I will be touching upon these aspects of *The God of Small Things* to show that it is definitely a postmodernist text.

As for experiments in language, Arundhati Roy applies language in a new and novel way. She uses lively words, phrases and expressions in her fictional work; for example, "He [one-armed man] could do only one thing at a time. If he held her, he couldn't kiss her. If he kissed her, he couldn't see her. If he saw her, he could not feel her" (1997, 4). The identity of the one-armed man is shrouded in mystery, and the language applied here becomes equally mysterious: "The God of Loss./ The God of Small Things./ The God of Goose Bumps and Sudden Smiles" (1997, 5 & 330). Roy's language becomes poetic and rhythmical here. So is the following passage about Baby Kochamma, a bulky woman seen urinating: "When the gurgling, bubbling sound came, she listened with her eyes. A yellow brook burbled through a mountain pass" (1997, 95). Keeping in mind Roy's experimentation with the English language, Anna Sujatha Mathai remarks: "Roy's sense of the language, her constant exploration and tasting, testing, balancing of it, adds to the originality and joy of the book" (*Indian Literature*: July-August 1997, 180). But Prof. C.D. Narasimhaiah finds fault with Roy's verbosity and long-windedness, with her use of words, lines and colours. He sharply observes: "To invoke the Sanskrit concept, her *atyukti* verbal excess offends against *auchitya* propriety, authenticity. In fact, this may be said pervasive through the whole book" (*The Literary Criterion*: Winter 1997, v).

The question of identity operates at a deeper level in *The God of Small Things,* for in face of a rigid social structure in India it is pretty difficult to identify oneself, tossed ever as one is by the inner conflicts of 'the self' and 'the other'. And this is the main problem in the way of lovemaking between a high-caste middle-aged woman and a low-caste young man (between Ammukutty and Velutha). This situation brings us closer to the question of feminism which pleads for women's emancipation in different walks of life, including economy and biology. Seen from this angle, Ammu is free to assert her sovereignty over her body and to give it to one of her liking. But when she does so, rigid social laws step in, and she is forcibly separated from her lover forever. Velutha is arrested and beaten badly in police custody and eventually dies. Ammu also dies of shock. Ammu is definitely a feminist whose needs of biology are totally ignored, and she, therefore, turns a rebel against the male-dominated society.

A third postmodernist Indian English novel is Aravind Adiga's *The White Tiger* (2008), which has also earned the Booker Prize for its author. Cast in the epistolary mode of writing, this novel highlights the binary of master/servant relationship, the struggle of a subordinate/subaltern for money and power, supported by the advancement of science and technology (one of Lyotard's 'master narratives').

The novel is postmodernist in nature and narrates the story of one Balram Halwai, son of a rickshaw-puller, who works as an assistant of the owner of a tea shop at the bus stop. He is unlettered, like his uncles and brothers. After a good deal of struggle, he gets the job of a chauffeur for Mr. Ashok, son of the landlord Stork, and his wife Madam Pinky, and in due course shifts to Delhi with pleasure and pride: "I'm going to Delhi in a car, an air-conditioned car" (Adiga: 2008, 112). Reaching Delhi, Balram becomes a bit bold and ambitious, and getting a chance for role-reversal, the servant (that he is) murders his master (Mr. Ashok) out of greed, for "seven hundred thousand rupees" (2008, 281) that he carries in a red bag to bribe the Coal Minister. With that money, he along with his cousin Dharam flees to the deep South, precisely to Bangalore, where he becomes a businessman, flourishes in his taxi-business, and fast turns from "a social entrepreneur to a business entrepreneur" (299).

He keeps bribing the police commissioner and enters a new business—the business of real estate—which has a bright future in Bengaluru. City of Bengaluru is well-known for its advanced science and technology, for excellence in computer and engineering. Its electronic gadgets and technological know-how serve to promote the consumerist culture in this city, a culture that gives Bengaluru its present identity. When Balram speaks of "this chandelier, and this silver laptop, and these twenty-six Toyota Qualis, with which he has been living so far or when he folds his future plan of starting 'real estate'" (319), with which he will live hereafter and mint huge money to establish an English language school to teach poor children in Bangalore to turn 'White Tigers' and ransack the whole city, he is neck-deep involved in pushing forth "the global economic system based on consumerism and capitalism" (N. Krishnaswamy *et al.* 2001; 2011, 19). Obviously, Balram still feels the pangs of poverty and misery of his past when he was a servant of Mr. Ashok and does not show any signs of repentance for killing his kind master. In reality, hunger for money, or what one might call the current craze for making fast bugs, makes Balram inhuman and cruel and he forgets all human relationships under the impact of 'consumerism and capitalism'. In this way, *The White Tiger* is a postmodernist novel highlighting the glamour of money and science.

III

To sum up: I have tried to show that 'postmodernism' may be interpreted in two ways: (1) as a historical period, and (2) as a way of life, a state of mind, and a series of social and cultural tendencies/attitudes. It may be regarded as a derivation from 'modernism' or a continuation of 'modernism' in certain matters as well as a discontinuation of certain modernist tendencies/ aptitudes. It is closely allied to poststructuralism in a linguistic analysis of a text (Saussure and Derrida), to postcolonialism in promoting orientalism (Edward Said), migrancy (Aijaz Ahmad), hybridity (Homi Bhabha), and subalternity of subjects (Gayatri Chakravorty Spivak and other feminists). The noted scholar, Jonathan Culler, rightly suggests: "Since the 1980s growing corpus of writings has debated questions about the relation between the hegemony of Western discourses and the possibilities of resistance, and about the formation of colonial and postcolonial subjects: hybrid subjects, emerging from the superimposition of conflicting languages and cultures" (1997; 2000, 130). Clearly, 'the superimposition of languages and cultures' has given birth to colonial power coming into contact with subject-nations and breeding the postmodernist atmosphere of pluculturalism and multiculturalism, of transnationalism and globalization, of consumerism and capitalism. Lack of the centre, loss of a sense of history and disbelief in the triumph of science (which give us Lyotard's suspicion of 'metanarratives') are some of the recognizable traits, among many others, of 'postmodernism' (and they have been outlined in the first section of this paper). I have then briefly yet pertinently examined three postmodernist texts—Rushdie's *Midnight's Children* (1981), Arundhati's *The God of Small Things* (1997), and Adiga's *The White Tiger* (2008)—to show how far 'post-modernism' has infiltrated into Indian English Fiction. I am also convinced that this area of investigation can be further extended by including a critical-cum-analytical study of the works of such writers as Amitav Ghosh, Githa Hariharan, Gita Mehta, Shashi Deshpande, Jhumpa Lahiri, Kiran Desai, and a few others, and hence leave it open-ended for a fuller debate and discussion about the impact of postmodernism on Indian English Fiction.

Works Cited

Adiga, Aravind. 2008. *The White Tiger*. Noida: HarperCollins Publishers.

Ahmad, Aijaz. 1992. *In Theory*. Oxford: Oxford University Press.

Barry, Peter. 2007. *Beginning Theory: An Introduction to Literary and Cultural Theory*. Manchester and New York: Manchester University Press.

Baudrillard, Jean. 1981; 1983. *Simulations*, tr. Paul Foss, Paul Patton and Philip Beitchman. New York: Semiotext(e).

Bertens, Hans. 1995. *The Idea of the Postmodern: A History*. London: Routledge.

———. 2001. *Literary Theory: The Basics*. London and New York: Routledge.

Bhabha, Homi K. 1994. *The Location of Culture*. London: Routledge.

Brooker, Peter. 1992. *Modernism/Postmodernism*. London: Longman.

Culler, Jonathan. 1996. *Literary Theory*. Oxford: Oxford University Press.

Eliot, T.S. 1922; 1963. *The Waste Land*. London: Faber and Faber.

———. 1963; 5th Imp. 1970. *Complete Poems*. London: Faber and Faber.

Hutcheon, Linda. 2006. *The Routledge Companion to Critical Theory*, eds. Simon Malpas and Paul Wake. London and New York: Routledge.

Kortenaar, Neil ten. 2004. *Self, Nation, Text in Salman Rushdie's 'Midnight Children'*. Montreal and London: McGrill-Queen's University Press.

Krishnaswamy, N. *et al.* 2001; 2011. *Contemporary Literary Theory*. Delhi: Macmillan Publishers India Ltd.

Loomba, Ania. 1998. *Colonialism/Postcolonialism*. London and New York: Routledge.

Lucy, Niall. 1997; 2002. *Postmodern Literary Theory: An Introduction*. Oxford and Malden: Blackwell Publishers Ltd.

Lyotard, Jean-Francois. 1984. *The Postmodern Condition*, tr. Geoff Bennington and Brian Massumi. Manchester and New York: Manchester University Press.

Mathai, Anna Sujatha. July August 1997. "Review of The God of Small Things", *Indian Literature*, Vol. XI, No. 4, 180.

Narasimhaiah, C.D. Winter 1997. "Editorial I—The Booker Prize: A Curse to Creativity: Arundhati Roy. The God of Small Things (1997)", *The Literary Criterion*. v.

Roy, Arundhati. 1997. *The God of Small Things*. New Delhi: IndiaInk.

Rushdie, Salman. 1981; 1995. *Midnight's Children*. London: Vintage Books.

———. 2008; 2009. *The Enchantress of Florence*. London: Vintage Books.

Yeats, W.B. 1994. "The Second Coming", *The Works of W.B. Yeats*. Hertfordshire, U.K.: The Wordsworth Poetry Library.

7

Magic Realism in Rushdie's *The Enchantress of Florence**

I

Earlier than *The Enchantress of Florence*, Rushdie had made ample use of magic realism in his *Midnight's Children* (1981). In the earlier novel, the narrator Saleem Sinai is born with a thousand other children at the stroke of midnight on August 15, 1947, coinciding with the birth of a new nation, and gifted with peculiar telepathic powers. Other children also show abnormal traits—for instance, there is a child who can travel through time, and yet another who can change sex at will. All the children have got one or the other magical property. Saleem is fated to have an avowed enemy in Shiva, another child born on the 15th August 1947 midnight. Shiva's character alludes to the Hindu mythology, but it can be stretched too far. It has been suggested that the rivalry between Saleem and Shiva is the rivalry between Brahma and Shiva in the matter of creation. Also, the reader discovers an amalgamation of Eastern (or Indian) and Western cultures in the text. Though the centrality of Saleem as the narrator of events can be questioned, the role of the *ayah* (nurse), Mary Pereira, who tells of supernatural events occurring in the streets of Bombay[1] and magical events picked up from the *Bible* (304) cannot be minimized. Moreover, the 'magical talk' of old Tai, the boatman, leaves a great impact on Saleem. Tai's talk definitely represents

* *Research and Criticism*, Journal of the Department of English, Banaras Hindu University, Varanasi, India. The paper is reprinted here with the permission of the Department of English, B.H.U.

the oral tradition of storytelling in Indian society. The oral serves the purpose of the written text. As for Mary, she stands for the fabulous in Saleem's narration, and is a superstitious Catholic and a devout reader of the *Bible*. The fantasy elements featuring prominently in her stories are a worldwide phenomenon and are usually associated with oral rumours and title-tattle (293) in distinct contrast to literate culture.

II

Like *Midnight's Children, The Enchantress of Florence* provides sufficient material of magic realism in its texture. *The Enchantress* contains flashes of dreams and omens, beliefs in magic and sorcery, and occasionally even the visions of the dead. In this novel, the narrative is woven around a tall, yellow-haired young European traveller called Mogor dell' Amore, *i.e.* the Mughal of Love, who tells at the court of Akbar, the great Mughal emperor, his remarkable tale that haunts the whole capital. This traveller claims to be the child of Kara Koz, 'Lady Black Eyes', a matchless bewitching beauty possessing the powers of enhancement and sorcery. Kara Koz deeply loves Argalia, a Florentine soldier. When Argalia returns to Florence along with Koz after many years of successful war and adventures outside, the whole city of Florence is simply mesmerized by her magnetic presence. Reviewing the novel for the *Tatler*, Geordie Grieg has appropriately remarked that it is "a boisterous tale piled high with sex and adventure and fantasy."[2]

The yarns of magic realism are marvelously woven in the novel around the memorable characters of Kara Koz and Argalia. These two characters show at time superhuman powers, extraordinary heroism, and dazzling charm and spell. As in Mark Twain's *The Adventures of Huckleberry Finn* (1885) the two important characters, Huck and Jim, display their unusual interest in the supernatural world and the prognostication of the future, in witches and ghosts, in dreams and omens,[3] so in *The Enchantress of Florence* Kara Koz and Argalia become the centre of attraction for their practice of magical powers and supernatural deeds at times.

In the very first chapter of *The Enchantress,* the cart-driver of the traveller frowns at the latter (who is carrying a secret with him to be revealed only to the emperor Akbar) and rebukes him thus: "Keep your secret.... Secrets are for children, and spies.... And for sorcerers.... And for lovers too. And kings"[4]. This speech is a pointer to the forthcoming events in the narrative, some of which are full of magic, sorcery and love. The same traveller, when he was in Florence, had met a conjurer who could make water disappear: "The conjurer filled a jug to the brim, muttered magic words, turned the jug over and, instead of liquid, fabric spilled forth, a torrent of coloured silken scarves" (9). A similar miraculous feat by the conjurer is mentioned in chapter two where he, by his magical powers, "transformed gold into smoke and yellow smoke back into gold" (15-16), and later vanished "the gloved bird and the birded glove" (17) from the band of Lord Hauksbank.

Occasionally Rushdie combines history and fantasy, the real and the unreal into one. In chapter 3, he speaks of Akbar as follows:

> Even the emperor succumbed to fantasy. Queens floated within his palaces like ghosts, Rajput and Turkish sultans playing catch-me-if-you-can. One of these royal personages did not really exist. She was an imaginary wife, dreamed up by Akbar in the way that lonely children dream up imaginary friends.... He gave her a name, Jodha, and no man dared gainsay him. (33)

Evidently, history is mixed with dream and fantasy here in a marvellous manner. An identical condition also prevails in chapter 4 where the nine Stars (*i.e. Navratna)* functioning so efficiently in the court of Akbar are recalled as those contributing to the wizardry of the renowned emperor: "With their help his wizardry would magic all the land, and the future, and all eternity. An emperor was a bewitcher of the real, and with such accomplices his witchcraft could not fail" (53).

It is a historical fact that Akbar loved Jodhabai more than the other queens, yet the fact is sugarcoated with the element of magic and sorcery. Rushdie remarkably describes the enchanting love-story of Jodha and Akbar:

> The other queens did not exist. Only she [Jodha] existed. She too was a sorceress. She was the sorceress of herself. There was only one man she needed to enchant, and he was here. He was not going to the other queens. He was coming to what pleased him. (62)

The historical reality is expressed here as a portion of sorcery and a matter of dreamland.

After a few initial chapters devoted mostly to the European traveller and the emperor Akbar, the story of Kara Koz and Argalia is skillfully narrated by the novelist. It was not that Kara Koz was the first enchantress of Florence; earlier than her there was Simonetta Cattaneo, who though married to Marco Vespucci, was shared by the whole city. Simonetta's husband bore all this indignity lest he should lost her, and hence he would say, with an idiotic innocence, that "such beauty is a public resource... like the river, or the gold in the treasury, or the fine light and air of Tuscany" (168). Simonetta's powers of enchantment were so great that she could "turn men into whatever she wanted them to be, gods or lapdogs or little barrels or footstools or, of course, lovers" (168-69).

In chapter 15, where the love-affair of Kara Koz with Argalia is narrated at some length and where Koz's Mirror (named Angelica) is introduced as her shadow, Koz is portrayed as under:

> She is the lady who loves you [Argalia], the Mirror said. She can charm the snakes from the ground and the birds from the trees and make them fall in love and she has fallen in love with you, so now you can have anything you desire. (283)

But Argalia has, initially, his reservations about her, as she had earlier left the company of her royal elder sister and fallen in love with Shah Ismail of Persia. Later Argalia got convinced of Koz's deep and unwavering love for him and for his heroic adventures and kept her with him wherever he went. And her spell upon him was of "the most benign kind" (341). Her extraordinary charm was simply disarming, not tricky like the mischievous activities of Hecate and three witches in Shakespeare's *Macbeth*.[5] Moreover, she was the most charming lady of the city, not of deserted places or woods. In this connection, the following extracts from the text can be quoted:

> Witches liked wandering in woods, everybody knew that, but the sylvan perambulation of Kara Koz and the Mirror were...no more than 'charming'. (342)
>
> Kara Koz created a hypnotic effect on the people about her. She was, in a way, an "incarnation of the Woman-wizard through whom the occult powers of all women were unleashed...." (352)

During Argalia's absence, in chapter 18, when he was leading the soldiers of Florence, on behalf of its Duke called Lorenzo de' Medici, in a battle against Francesco Maria, the Duke of Urbino, Lorenzo started making advances towards Koz. Meanwhile Lorenzo caught a strange disease that ate his body away like a hungry animal starting with the genitals and working outwards from there. The Florentines blamed Koz for his deadly disease and subsequent death. She was called a witch: "Witch. She bewitched him. He lay with the witch and sickened and died. He was not sick before. Witchcraft. She gave him the Devil's disease. Witch, witch, witch" (374). As a result, a riot broke out against her, and the timely arrival of the war wounded Argalia and his trusted men helped her (and the Mirror) escape safely. But before her departure, she expressed her deep love for Argalia once again—"I have loved you like no other man", to which the latter replied by saying "You have been the love of my life" (381). Immediately afterwards, Argalia, the brave great general, breathed his last.

In the last chapter (19th), we come to know that the Mughal of Love, the yellow-haired European traveller, confides his so-called 'secret' to Akbar in such a powerful way that he is made the advisor and confidant of the emperor. Akbar is deeply affected by the enchanting story of Kara Koz and he starts dreaming of her day and night: "Her sorcery. Which not even he, the emperor, could resist" (402). Like the people of Sikri, Akbar inescapably falls into her snares. She comes to haunt him, to ensure him, to dislodge the historical queen Jodhabai, and to capture her place as his companion hereafter. Having slipped into the world of fantasy, of unreality, Kara Koz comes to haunt Akbar's palace, even his heart and mind, as a more real being than "that flesh-and-blood woman of the past..." (418). At the close of the novel, Mogor dell' Amore, the traveller reveals: "My mother was Kara Koz, your grandfather's [Babar's] sister, the great enchantress, and she learned how to stop time" (430). That night, Kara Koz appears before the emperor and discloses to him that Amore is not her son (which he believes to be) but the son of her Mirror's daughter, and that she has now come "to command his dreams, usurping another woman's place in his *khayal*, his godlike, omnipotent fancy" (442). Thus, Kara Koz becomes eventually a creature of fancy and fantasy, no more a woman of flesh and blood; in other words, she slips from the mundane world into the world of magic reality.

III

From the foregoing observations it is obvious that *The Enchantress of Florence,* like its predecessor *Midnight's Children*, is replete with fantastical and magical details. The novel provides sufficient fanciful and alluring material that may, at times, transgress our sense of rationality and conviction. In the fast-changing academic world, literary theories may emerge, get modified, or even be rejected, and the fate of magic(al) realism is, by and large, no different. Speaking of the future of magic realism, Maggie Ann Bowers remarks thus: "Ultimately, the problems of magical realism are inherent in its contradictory and multi-perspectival form and this may, in the future, be its nemesis" (123). Another scholar, Brenda Cooper also points out the contradictions of magical realism, and one of them is that writers like Rushdie "walk a political tightrope between capturing...reality and providing precisely the exotic escape from reality desired by some of their Western readership" (32). Contradictions are accepted, but the presentability of reality, including history, depends on the skillful handling of the narrative by individual writers, and Rushdie as a magic realist beautifully blends the magical lore with history, as in *The Enchantress of Florence*, rendering it an enchanting fictional narrative.

Notes

1. Rushdie, Salman (1981). *Midnight's Children,* London: Picador, p. 293. Other references to this novel are absorbed in the body of the paper itself.
2. Cited from the back blurb of Salman Rushdie's *The Enchantress of Florence.*
3. For details on the use of magic in *Huckleberry Finn*, one can look up Daniel Hoffman's article "Black Magic–and White–in *Huckleberry Finn", Twentieth Century Views* (1963), ed. Henry Nash Smith. New Jersey: Prentice-Hall Inc., p. 102. This paper also appeared in *American Literature*, an internationally reputed literary journal of America. This critic observes that for Huck "the omens are an acknowledgement of the fact of death" (102), and about Jim he remarks that "Divination with a hairball from the stomach of an ox is a Negro belief in voodoo origin" (109).
4. Rushdie, Salman. *The Enchantress of Florence.* p. 7. Other references to the novel are indicated in the paper itself.
5. *Cf.* Shakespeare, William (ELBS ed. 1964). *Macbeth*, Act 3, Sc. 4, II. 3-9; cited from Shakespeare, *The Complete Works.* London & Glasgow: ELBS & Collins, p. 102. These lines are quoted below for a ready reference:

   How did you dare
   To trade and traffic with Macbeth
   In riddles and affairs of death;
   And I, the mistress of your charms,
   The close contriver of all harms,
   Was never call'd to bear my part,
   Or show the glory of our art?

Works Cited

Abrams, M.H. *A Glossary of Literary Terms.* 7th ed. Singapore: Thomas Heinle, 1999. Print.

Bowers, Maggie Ann. *Magic(al) Realism.* London & New York: Routledge, 2004. Print.

Cooper, Brenda, *Magical Realism in West African Fiction: Seeing with a Third Eye.* London Routledge, 1998. Print.

Riemenschneider, Dieter. "An Enchanting Story. *The Journal of Contemporary Literature* 1.1 (2009): 131-34. Print.

Rushdie, Salman, *Midnight's Children*, 1981. London: Picador, 1981. Print.

_____. *The Enchantress of Florence.* 2008. London: Vintage, 2009. Print.

8

Myth, History, Tradition and Modernity in Indian English Drama

Drama is designated as the fifth Veda and defined as *drishya kavya* (visible poetry). Its affinity with the Veda renders it divine and knowledgeable, whereas its visibility on the stage makes it different from poetry or any other form of literature. If poetry is a by-product of imagination, drama is a by-product of visibility and audibility[1] on a theatrical stage. Kenneth Pickering, a noted drama scholar, thinks that the majority of successful playwrights ever strive for "the performance of their plays"[2] on the stage.

The very origin of drama in ancient India is steeped in myth which is defined as a story that "narrates in an imaginative and symbolic manner the total and basic structure upon which a culture rests."[3] It is mentioned in the first chapter of the *Nātyaśāstra* that the Creator of the Universe, Brahma, wished to perform a drama in heaven, but sensing some foreseeable trouble from the demons, he entrusted the task to Bharata, who along with his hundred sons, enacted it to the delight and blessings of the gods. The title of the play was *The Defeat of Demons*. The demons could not relish it and indulged in destructive activities. Thus, the beginning of Indian drama has been fraught with dangers and challenges.

Sanskrit drama faced these dangers and challenges squarely and emerged strong in due course of time. The dramatic writings of Bhasa, Kalidas and Bhavabhuti and a few others put it on a high pedestal, reminding us of the flowering of drama in ancient Greece, in the hands of Aeschylus, Euripides and Sophocles.

But the Greek drama followed the tradition of Tragedy and the Indian drama the tradition of Comedy (for instance, Kalidas's *Abhijnanasakuntalam*).

Indian English drama has been indigenous in content but alien in expression. It is a literary variety of transplantation in expression. That's why Indian drama mostly flourished in regional languages like Marathi, Bengali, Tamil and Kannada. Usually, the participation of the audience is made possible through the mother tongue, not through a foreign tongue. Evidently, drama is a "composite art involving the playwright, the actor and the audience in a commonly shared, and even created, artistic experience"[4], and hence calls for a total commitment of these various persons to create a desired lasting impact. Indian English drama is, however, deprived of this privilege.

Indian English drama, by its very nature, could not plant itself in the Indian ethos[5]. India has been a rich storehouse of myths and legends, of folktales and oral customs, of historical events and cultural heritage, but most of the Indian English dramatists, barring possibly Girish Karnad and Asif Currimbhoy, have failed to make use of them. Rabindranath Tagore and Sri Aurobindo, who were deeply laved in Indian culture, mythology and history, tried their hands at them but could not resolve the dilemma or conflict between the inner and outer worlds. But Karnad in his *Yayati, Tughlaq, Hayavadana* and *Nagamandala* and Currimbhoy in his *Goa*, *Inquilab* and *The Hungry Ones* have achieved this difficult task.

And a third reason for the paucity of Indian English drama is its unsuitability in performing on the stage.[6] Because of this deficiency, it has suffered immensely in producing the impressive theatrical effects. This fact has impelled K.R. Srinivasa Iyengar to remark: "Modern Indian dramatic writing in English is neither rich in quantity, nor, on the whole, of high quality."[7] M.K. Naik thinks in the self-same direction when he states that "A play, in order to communicate fully and become living dramatic experience...needs a real theatre and a live audience.... It is precisely the lack of these essentials that has hamstrung Indian drama in English all along."[8] We must mention here that English drama flourished so luxuriantly during the Elizabethan age because a number of talented writers, including William Shakespeare (1565-1616), were busy in producing their delightful plays for "a real theatre and a live audience."

But it should not be construed from the above-noted observations that Indian English drama has remained a non-starter and has become incurably crippled. Right from the early nineteenth century, with the publication of Krishna Mohan Banerji's *The Persecuted or Dramatic Scenes Illustrative of the Present State of Hindoo Society in Calcutta* (1831; the first Indian play in English), charming plays have been written by a number of gifted writers, like R.N. Tagore, Sri Aurobindo, T.P. Kailasam, A.S.P. Ayyar, Harindranath Chattopadhyay and Bharati Sarabhai in the pre-independence era and Asif Currimbhoy, Girish Karnad, Badal Sircar, Lakhan Deb, Gurcharan Das, Vijay Tendulkar, Mohan Rakesh, Mahesh Dattani and Manjula Padmanabhan in the post-independence era. In my paper, I have tried to analyze and assess the contributions of these writers in the light of myth, tradition and modernity to be found in Indian English drama.

In the nineteenth century, Michael Madhusudan Dutt wrote such plays as *Ratnavali* (1858), *Sarmista* (1859), and *Is This Called Civilization ?* (1871), first in Bengali and then translated them into English. Ram Kinoo Dutt also produced his *Manipura Tragedy* in 1839.

Some of the outstanding dramatists of the pre-Independence period were Rabindranath Tagore (1861-1941), Sri Aurobindo (1872-1950), T.P. Kailasam (1885-1946), and ASP Ayyar (1899-1963). Those who are interested in them should read their plays for pleasure and profit. Tagore has written more than a dozen plays, and his *Muktadhara* (The Waterfall), *The Post Office* and *The King of the Dark Chamber* had earned great popularity. Similarly, some of the plays of Sri Aurobindo like *Perseus the Deliverer, Vasavadatta, Rodogune, The Viziers of Bassora* and *Eric the King of Norway* have become quite famous. T.P. Kailasam is well-known for his plays like *The Burden* (1933), *Fulfilment* (1933), *The Purpose* (1944), *The Curse or Karma* (1946) and *Keechaka* (1949). S.K. Bhatta informs us that Kailasam has written about thirteen more English plays, unfinished and unpublished.[9] And A.S.P. Ayyar has also made substantial contributions to drama with his *In the Clutch of the Devil* (1926), *Sita's Choice and Other Plays* (1935), *The Slave of Ideas & Other Plays* (1941), and *The Trial of Science and Murder of Humanity* (1942), and these plays deal with "contemporary problems and situations."[10]

Two names must be mentioned here as recognized writers of Indian English drama before India's independence: Harindranath Chattopadhyay and Bharti Sarabhai. While Chattopadhyay was a prolific writer[11], Sarabhai has produced just two plays—*The Well of the People* (1943) and *Two Women* (1952). Most of Chattopadhyay's plays expose the evils in Indian society, but they lack "suspense and concentration."[12] And Sarabhai's plays present "different facets of Indian womenhood"[13] in a forceful manner.

The post-independence scenario (after 1947) has been a bit more heartening. Asif Currimbhoy, Girish Karnad, Badal Sircar, Lakhan Deb, Gurcharan Das and Vijay Tendulkar have shown greater control of the tool and skilled application of language and dialogue. Leaving aside G.V. Desani whose play *Hali* (1950) displays originality of approach, vividness of imagery and powerful portrayal of characters like Hali and Rooh (an evasive beauty), we directly come to Asif Currimbhoy who has produced over two dozen plays to date on a variety of themes—social, political, religious, psychological, national and international. Like *Hali,* Currimbhoy's plays have been staged in both India and abroad. They are of topical interest, and some of them like *Goa* (1964), *Inquilab* (1970), *The Refugee* (1971), *Sonar Bangla* (1972), The *Miracle Seed* (1973) have become quite popular. Currimbhoy's appeal lies in his use of natural and simple language, in keeping with the occasion and the character in a particular play. Faubion Bowers judiciously suggests that "Currimbhoy is India's authentic voice in the theatre."[14]

History plays an important role in Currimbhoy's dramas with Indian setting, for example in *The Captives* (1963), *Goa* (1964), *An Experiment with Truth* (1969), *Inquilab* (1970), *The Refugee* (1971), *Sonar Bangla* (1972), and *The Dissident MLA* (1974). So also, it enacts a great part in Girish Karnad's *Tughlaq* (1964) and *The Dreams of Tipu Sultan* (2004). A highly gifted writer that Karnad is, he bases his *Tughlaq* on the history of Sultan Muhammad-bin-Tughlaq of the fourteenth century. This ruler of Delhi was, in reality, an idealist visionary and a demagogue, a farsighted man and an impartial ruler. Speaking of him, Karnad remarks that Tughlaq was "certainly the most brilliant individual ever to ascend the throne of Delhi, and also one of the biggest failures."[15] The play is also an allegory of Nehru and the Nehruvian era. As regards *The Dreams of Tipu Sultan,* it represents the historical happenings during the reign of Tipu, the Tiger of Mysore, and the British colonial reflections on it. Tipu challenges the imperialist British on the battlefield, but outmaneuvered and killed. However, as O.P. Budholia puts it, Karnad "succeeds in vindicating the character of Tipu as a soldier who fought and died for the sake of India as a nation...."[16]

Like Currimbhoy and Karnad, Lakhan Deb has also produced two memorable historical plays titled *Tiger's Claw* (1967) and *Murder at the Prayer Meeting* (1976). The play *Tiger's Claw* powerfully portrays Shivaji's killings of Afzal Khan. K.R.S. Iyengar remarks that the theme of the play has "elements of pure drama...."[17] And the play *Murder at the Prayer Meeting* deals with the gruesome assassination of Mahatma Gandhi by Nathu Ram Godse on 30th January 1948 when the former was coming out of his prayers in Delhi. In texture and technique, it is comparable to T.S. Eliot's *Murder in the Cathedral* (1935). O.P. Bhatnagar is of the view that the play provides "a better model of conduct in human values than *Murder in the Cathedral.*"[18] Another dramatist, Gurcharan Das, dwells on a historical event in his *Larins Sahib* (1970). This play highlights the happenings in the Punjab of 1946-47 when Ranjit Singh, called *Sher-è-Punjab*, died and Lord Harding, the then Governor-General of India, appointed Henry Lawrence as the Resident in the court of Dalip Singh, the twelve-year-old son of Ranjit Singh. Lawrence, nicknamed as Larins Sahib, was initially soft to the subjects and to the Queen (who in good faith offered him the precious Kohinoor for safe-keeping), but became dictatorial and power-drunk later on. He even dared to kiss the Queen in a passionate mood and refused to return her the crowned Kohinoor. Commenting on the play, C.V. Venugopal writes:

"*Larins Sahib*...can boast of enough elements that ensure great success on the stage."[19]

Some other dramatists of historical and political import are: Santha Rama Rau (*A Passage to India,* a dramatized version of E.M. Forster's novel published in 1960), Dilip Hero (*To Anchor a Cloud*, 1972), K.A. Abbas (*Barrister at Law*, 1977), and Manohar Malgonkar (*Lines of Mars*, 1978).

Some dramatists have dealt with the life, character and achievements of Mahatma Gandhi, such as K.A. Abbas, Lakhan Deb, and K.A. Rangappa (*Gandhi's Sadhna*, 1969). M.V. Rama Sarma portrays the events leading to the assassination of Gandhiji in his *The Mahatma.*

We also have few other dramatists who have dwelt on the freedom struggle of India and the need of national integration. V.K. Gokak's *The Goddess Speaks* (1948), D.M. Borgaonkar's *The Great Coward and the Refugee* (contained in *One-Act-Plays,* 1957), R. Javanthinathan's *Guardianship of India* are all on chaos and confusion, loot and arson, bloodshed and butchery prevalent in the days of freedom struggle. And J.M. Billimoria's *My Sons* (1963), Hussenali Chagla's *The Mussulman* (1966), and Hushmat Sozrekashme's *Vikramjeet* (1970) underline the importance of the Hindu-Muslim unity in the aftermath of partition.

M.V. Rama Sarma is a forceful voice in Indian English drama. He combines eastern and western trends in his plays. While his *Shakuntala* and *Urvashi* are written in the Sanskrit tradition, his *Youth and Crabbed Age, Like to Like* and *The Busy World* are cast in the Western tradition. His plays, included in *Collected Plays* (1982), recall Sri Aurobindo to us. The impact of G.B. Shaw is clearly felt upon him in his Western plays. He has written eleven plays in total and some of them are "loose in structure and weak in characterization."[20]

Pratap Sharma has produced two plays on the theme of sex and exploitation of woman. His first play, *The Professor Has a War Cry* (1970), highlights the desertion of a wife by a Professor and her successive rape by a Muslim and an Englishman. His second play, *A Touch of Brightness* (1973), portrays the red-light area in Bombay where the flesh trade is carried on. M.K. Naik commends this play for its "thematic boldness."[21]

Tradition is defined as "the inherited past" or something that is "passed down from generation to generation through custom and practice."[22] In the Indian context, it is the Sanskrit tradition that has ever enlivened and enriched our arts and literature. T.S. Eliot thinks that a good and great tradition "is never dead and that it lives in the present."[23] As contrasted to tradition. modernity or modernism in literature marks "a breaking away from established rules, traditions and conventions, fresh ways of looking at man's position and function in the universe and many (in some cases remarkable) experiments in form and style."[24]

Indian tradition and culture have been carried forward in Indian English drama by Tagore, Aurobindo, Gokak and a few others like D.D. Roy (*Sri Chaitanya*, 1950), V.V.S. Iyengar (*Rāmarājya*, 1952), Mathuram Bhoothalingam (*Alone in Ayodhya*), Smt. K.B. Mathur (*Mother and Child*, 1960), and Sadar Joshi (*Acharya Drona*, 1963). These playwrights have gone to the *Rāmāyana* and the *Mahābhārata* for their themes. As briefly mentioned earlier, the Indian tradition begins with the Sanskrit plays. The distinguished Sanskrit scholar, A.B. Keith rightly points out: "Indian tradition, preserved in the *Nātyaśāstra*, the oldest of the texts of the theory of drama, claims for the drama divine origin, and a close connection with the sacred *Vedas* themselves."[25] The noted historian, A.L. Basham, also expresses similar views: "The origin of the Indian theatre is still obscure. It is certain, however, that even in the Vedic period dramatic performances of some kind were given...."[26] Here it must be mentioned that several plays (running into ten Acts) and playlets (limited to only on Act) have survived in Sanskrit. The chief Sanskrit dramatists were: Ashvaghosa, Bhasa, Kalidas, Bhavabhuti and Śudrak. The plays of these celebrated writers have become an invaluable treasure of our literary heritage.

Modernity is reflected in the works of such writers as Girish Karnad, Badal Sircar, Mohan Rakesh and Vijay Tendulkar. Surprisingly, these writers are largely writing in their own regional language; for example, Girish Karnad in Kannada, Badal Sircar in Bengali, Mohan Rakesh in Hindi and Vijay Tendulkar in Marathi. These playwrights are innovative and experimentalist to a great extent in their content and technique. Karnad is well-known as an explorer of myths and folklore in his plays like *Yayati* (1961; his first play), *Naga-Mandala* (1988), *The Fire and the Rain* (1995), and *Bali: The Sacrifice* (2004). Badal Sircar's *Evam Indrajit* (1974), translated into English by Girish Karnad, is a remarkable work on human predicament. As we know, Badal is the founder of the Third Theatre, which steers itself clear of the theatre of an urban intelligentsia in Calcutta and the folk-theatre of the village. Mohan Rakesh's writings in Hindi dwell on the impact of modernization on different human relationships. He is not a prolific writer, but his contributions are substantial. His full-length plays—*One Day in Ashadha* (1958), *The Great Swans of the Waves* (1962), and *Halfway House* (1969)—and his short plays opened up new vistas for Hindi Drama. His *One Day in Ashadha*, a historical play, intensely explores man-woman relationship through the characters of Kalidas and his beloved Mallika. As for Vijay Tendulkar, he is a social realist to the core. His Play, *Shantata! Court Chalu Ahe* (1970), in Marathi was later translated into English and became immediately successful. Commenting on this play, Ramesh P. Panigrahi writes that it "is the first post-colonialist play in its implications. It presents a metaphorical trial between the humanists and the anti-humanists...."[27]

Two other promising playwrights of modernistic mindset must be mentioned now and here—Mahesh Dattani and Manjula Padmanabhan. Dattani has written plays like *Where There's a Will* (1988), *Dance Like a Man* (1989), *Tara* (1990), *Bravely Fought the Queen* (1991), *Final Solutions* (1992-93), and *Thirty Days in September* (2001). Stephen Bruckner remarked in *The New York Times* that Dattani was a "canny and facile writer...."[28] And Manjula created a stir in the literary world with her *Harvest* (2003), which bagged the prestigious Onassis Award. This play deals with a miserable family dwelling in a single room in a chawl of Mumbai.

The above account of Indian English drama augurs well for the future growth of this *genre*. The present essay/paper sharply focuses on Myth, History, Tradition and Modernity in Indian English drama, and this renders it all the more challenging and rewarding.

Notes

1. Of the various gifts received by Bharata after a successful performance of drama like the auspicious banner (*dhvaja*) by Indra, an umbrella by Surya, a fan by Vāyu, a *kutilaka* by Brahma, a golden pitcher by Varuna, *Siddhi* (success) by Shiva, a lion-seat by Vishnu, a crown by Kubera—visibility and audibility are offered to him by Saraswati. (*Nātyasāstra*, I. 60-61).

   —Kapila Vatsyayan, *Bharata: The Nātyaśāstra* (New Delhi: Sahitya Akademi, 2005 rpt.), p. 15.
2. Kenneth Pickering, *Studying Modern Drama* (Houndmills, Basingstoke, Hampshire: Palgrave Macmillan, 1988 & 2003).
3. Grolier, *Encyclopedia of Knowledge,* Mod-Nuc. 13 (Grolier International, 1999), p. 191.
4. M.K. Naik & S. Mokashi-Punekar, *Perspectives on Indian Drama in English* (Madras: O.U.P., 1977), p. ix.
5. A.N. Dwivedi, *Studies in Contemporary Indian English Drama* (Ludhiana & New Delhi: Kalyani Publishers, 1999), p. 1.
6. *Ibid*., p. 2.
7. K.R. Srinivasa Iyengar, *Indian Writing in English,* 4th ed. (New Delhi: Sterling Publishers Pvt. Ltd., 1984), p. 226.
8. M.K. Naik, "The Achievement of Indian Drama in English", *Perspectives on Indian Drama in English* (1977), p. 181.
9. S. Krishna Bhatta, "Kailasam's English Plays", *Perspectives on Indian Drama in English,* eds., Naik & Punekar, p. 86.
10. A.N. Dwivedi, *op. cit*., p. 8.
11. Harindranath Chattopadhyay's plays are generally classified under four heads: (1) devotional plays, (2) social plays, (3) historical plays, and (4) miscellaneous plays. In the first category, we have such plays as *Raidas*, *Chokha Mela*, *Eknath Pundalik, Sakubai, Jayadeva* and *Tukaram*; in the second, we have *The Window, The Parrot, The Coffin, The Evening Lamp,* and *The Sentry's Lantern*; in the third, we have *Siddhartha, the Man of Peace*, *The Saint, The Sleep Awakened, Perfume of Earth,* and *Kannappan or The Hunter of Kalahasti*. For more details, see G.S. Balaram Gupta's article "The Plays of Harindranath Chattopadhyay", *Perspectives on Indian Drama in English,* eds. Naik & Puneker, pp. 115-18.
12. S.K. Bhatt, *Indian English Drama: A Critical Study* (New Delhi: Sterling Publishers Pvt. Ltd., 1987), p. 52.

13. *Ibid.*, p. 58.
14. Faubion Bowers, "Introduction", *Asif Currimbhoy's Plays* (New Delhi: Oxford & IBH, n.d.), p. xii.
15. Girish Karnad, "Introduction to *Three Plays*", rpt. in *The Plays of Girish Karnad*, ed. Jaydipsinh Dodiya (New Delhi: Prestige Books, 1999), p. 27.
16. O.P. Budholia, *Girish Karnad: History and Folklore* (Delhi: B.R. Publishing Corporation, 2011), p. 136.
17. K.R. Srinivasa Iyengar, *Indian Writing in English*, 4th ed. (New Delhi: Sterling Publishers Pvt. Ltd., 1984), p. 246.
18. O.P. Bhatnagar, "Lakhan Deb's *Murder at the Prayer Meeting* and T.S. Eliot's *Murder in the Cathedral*: A Comparative Study", *Meerut Journal of Comparative Language and Literature*, I, No. 2, (1988), p. 73.
19. C.V. Venugopal, "*Larins Sahib*", *Perspectives on Indian Drama in English*, eds. Naik & Punekar, p. 179.
20. A.N. Dwivedi, *op. cit.*, p. 14.
21. M.K. Naik, *A History of Indian English Literature* (New Delhi: Sahitya Akademi, 1982), p. 261.
22. J.A. Cuddon, rev. by C.E. Preston, *The Penguin Dictionary of Literary Terms and Literary Theory* (Harmondsworth & London: Penguin Books, 1999 ed.), p. 925.
23. T.S. Eliot, "Tradition and the Individual Talent", *The Sacred Wood* (London: Faber & Faber, 1920), p. 53.
24. J.A. Cuddon, *op. cit.*, pp. 515-16.
25. A.B. Keith, *The Sanskrit Drama* (Delhi: Motilal Banarsidass, 1992), p. 12.
26. A.L. Basham, *The Wonder That Was India* (New Delhi: Rupa & Co., 1987), pp. 434-35.
27. Ramesh P. Panigrahi, "Game as Text and Text as Game: Tendulkar's *Silence! The Court Is In Session*", *Studies in Contemporary Indian English Drama* (1999), ed. A.N. Dwivedi, pp. 124-25.
28. Cited from Neeru Tandon, *Perspectives and Challenges in Indian English Drama* (New Delhi: Atlantic Publishers, 2006), p. 93.

9

Contemporary Indian English Poetry: A Study in Culture and Identity

First of all, Contemporary Indian English poetry need not be associated with post-Independence Indian English poetry, though it is convenient to some in terms of history. The terms 'contemporary' and 'contemporaneity' bring Indian English poetry closer to our times. These terms unequivocally suggest what is 'current' or 'in currency' or 'in fashion', and thereby, hint at the latest in theme and style, in form and idiom. *Longman Dictionary of Contemporary English* (1978 & 2003) offers two meanings of the term 'contemporary': one, 'belonging to the present time', and two, 'happening or done in the same period of time' (395). If we slightly change the title of this essay/paper and replace 'Contemporary Indian English Poetry' by 'Indian English Poetry Today', the cobwebs of confusion about the term 'contemporary' will be cleared to a large extent.

Indian English poetry is unquestionably an offshoot of Indian English literature, which arose out of adverse circumstances. India was then groaning, like a tightly chained lion inside an unbreakable cage, under British rule. Many poets, such as Henry Derozio, Rabindranath Tagore, Sri Aurobindo, Sarojini Naidu, and Harindranath Chattopadhyay raised their voice against British cruelty and sang songs in honour of Mother India. Because of their efforts as well as the efforts of our valiant and visionary statesmen like Tilak, Gokhale, Lala Lajpat Rai, Gandhi,

Nehru, Subhash, Patel and others, India attained independence on 15th August 1947. By that time, Derozio, the National Bard of Modern India and R.N. Tagore, the recipient of the Nobel Prize for Literature in 1913, were no more. Sri Aurobindo, the torchbearer of Indian culture and identity, had retired from active politics and taken to the course of meditation and *yoga* in the Pondicherry *ashram*. And Sarojini Naidu, the Nightingale of India, had plunged headlong into politics and become the first Governor of Uttar Pradesh.

Culturally speaking, three poets are simply outstanding: Toru Dutt (1856-77), Rabindranath Tagore (1861-1941), and Sri Aurobindo (1872-1950). All the three poets belonging to the older generation, to 'the age of Romantics' (as P. Lal and the Writers Workshop group later called them), had studied Sanskrit in original and put their knowledge of Sanskrit to a creative use when they came to composing their own poetry. K.R.S. Iyengar thinks that Toru's readings in the *Ramayana,* the *Mahabharata*, the *Vishnu Purana*, the *Gita*, and also *Shakuntalam* gave "her woman's imagination free play" (1973, 2nd ed.: 63). Toru's *Ancient Ballads and Legends of Hindustan* (1882) is a remarkable collection of nine ballads and legends culled from the two great Hindu epics. It wonderfully interprets the cultural soul of India to the West, prompting Sir Edmund Gosse to comment that this collection of poems "will be ultimately found to constitute Toru's chief legacy to posterity" ("Introductory Memoir", *Ancient Ballads and Legends of Hindustan.* London: Kegan Paul & Co., 1882, xxiii).

Rabindranath Tagore's *Gitanjali* took the literary world by storm on its appearance in 1912. Tagore reached England with its manuscript, which was translated into English from the original Bengali by the poet himself. He showed it to his old friend William Rothenstein, a renowned artist, and Rothenstein gave it to W.B. Yeats, Stopford, C.F. Andrews, Henry Nevinson, and several other *literati*, who were all enthralled with its profundity of thought, subtlety of rhythm, delicacy of touch, and inventiveness of metre. Yeats was so much mesmerized that he carried the manuscript with him wherever he went and read it in railway trains, on the top of omnibuses and in restaurants.

Yeats recommended it for the Nobel Prize, and Tagore's *Gitanjali* deservedly got it. Later, Yeats wrote an excellent Introduction to this collection of 103 divine songs. He called it "the work of a supreme culture", wherein the songs "appear as much the growth of the common soil as the grass and the rushes" ("Introduction", *Gitanjali*. Madras: Macmillan Co. of India, 1973, xi). He further commented on it thus: "A whole people, a whole civilization, immeasurably strange to us, seems to have been taken up into this imagination..." ("Introduction", xiii-xiv).

Then comes Sri Aurobindo, the Sage of Pondicherry, with his meditative and mystic poetry. He experimented with this kind of poetry in a number of poems before he wrote *Savitri* in twelve books comprising about 24,000 lines, full of symbols and visions. Some of his smaller poems steeped in mysticism are: "Invitation" (which was actually composed in 1908, in the Alipur Jail where he had had the ineffable mystic joy of Vasudeva Darshan), "Who", "The Rishi", "The Birth of Sin", "To the Sea", "The Vedantin's Prayer", "The Bird of Fire", "Trance", "Jivanmukta", "Thought the Paraclete", "Transformation", and "Rose of God". These smaller poems have a depth of thought and are a prelude to *Savitri* (1950-51), which is directly based on the story of Savitri and Satyavan to be found in the *Mahabharata*. In this epic cast in blank verse and grand style, the old legend of Savitri is transformed into a symbol, and in the course of her evolution "Savitri the girl-wife becomes the Mother Might and Vanquisher of Death, and also the Creatrix of the Life Divine on Earth" (K.R.S. Iyengar, *Sri Aurobindo: An Introduction*. Mysore: Rao & Raghavan, 1961, 47). Like Homer and Milton, Sri Aurobindo tends to be eloquent and sublime in his utterances, and his *Savitri* becomes "an excellent exposition of 'Overhead' poetry" (See my book, *Indo-Anglian Poetry,* 1979 & 1987, 154-61).

II

In case of a nation-state, language, literature, race, history and geography play a vital role. All these things combine to promote a national culture. In his seminal book, *The Wretched of the Earth* (1961), Frantz Fanon writes: "A culture is first and foremost the expression of a nation, its preferences, its taboos, its models" (177). Scholars have variously interpreted 'national culture'; for instance, Homi K. Bhabha has equated it with 'global cosmopolitanism' in his bright book *The Location of Culture* ("Introduction", 1994, xvi), and Pankaj Mishra has bracketed it with "modernize or perish" slogan (*Ibid.*). At a time when globalization is marching ahead with rapid strides, national culture has turned transnational and transcultural. Bhabha's 'global cosmopolitanism' is a pointer to this fact. Now, culture (-s) has (have) crossed the boundaries of a nation and become global and transnational. And transnational culture has a two-way traffic, and it operates at both international and local levels, as pointed out by Bhabha. At the international level, multinational companies are now setting up malls and supermarkets the world over, breeding pluculturalism and multiculturalism and creating an environment favourable for 'capitalist culture', and at the local or national level minorities living in backward or tribal areas are getting more exposure and reaching out to international markets with their products and handicrafts. With greater exposure, some members of the minorities become computer engineers, technicians, and entrepreneurs and medicos. That's why Bhabha states that "Globalization must always begin at home" (1994, xv). Some scholars like Bhabha and Tariq Modood talk of 'cultural hybridity' which is seen operating in the present-day world around.

The question of identity is also beset with speculations and challenges. Critics like Stuart Hall and Paul Du Gay have raised the question of 'cultural identity' in their edited book, *Questions of Cultural Identity* (1996 & 2008), in a forceful manner. They are of the view that identity is "the formation of subjectivity" and that it is akin to a sense of "belonging" ("Introduction", 9). Stuart Hall, in particular, thinks that the question of identity operates within the ambit of relationship of the 'self' to 'the other'. He equates 'identity' with 'identification' (*Ibid.*, 2). Elsewhere, in an article titled "Cultural Identity and Diaspora", which is included in Padmini Mongia's edited book, *Contemporary Postcolonial Theory* (1996), Stuart Hall states:

> There are at least two different ways of thinking about 'cultural identity'. The first position defines 'cultural identity' in terms of one shared culture, a sort of collective 'one true self', hiding inside the many other, more superficial or artificially imposed 'selves', which people with a shared history and ancestry hold in common. (110-11)

Continuing his argument further in the same article, Stuart Hall remarks:

> Cultural identity, in this second sense, in a matter of 'becoming' as well as of 'being'. It belongs to the future as much as to the past. It is not something which already exists, transcending place, time, history and culture. Cultural identities come from somewhere, have histories. But, like everything which is historical, they undergo constant transformation. (112)

This second view of cultural identity, as Stuart Hall holds, is much less familiar, and more unsettling (113).

The question of identity, especially in the second sense of Stuart Hall, has always occupied the minds of Hindu sages and seers, who have articulated it is their own characteristic way: 'Aham Brahma' ('I am Brahman'), 'Tat Tvam Asi' ('That thou art') are the famous Vedic and Upanishadic sayings. In the Western context, the great Greek philosopher, Socrates, has passionately pleaded for the motto 'Know thyself'. If religion is a matter of belief; nation, a construct of history and geographical boundaries; society, a formation of races and communities, identity is the essence of identification and recognition. Thus, we have religious identity, national identity, social identity, and cultural identity as well as individual identity and linguistic identity.

III

So long I have been trying either to discover the background of Indian English Poetry or to do some justice to the subject of this paper. Hereafter, I will take a headlong plunge into a discussion of Contemporary Indian English Poetry. At once, two names spring up in my mind: Nissim Ezekiel (1924-2004) and

P. Lal (1929-2010), who are not only historically important, appearing as they do in the 1950s, but also poetically relevant being conscious of their culture and identity. In this context, I would like to draw your attention to Ezekiel's poem "Background, Casually". Consisting of three sections, the poem is quite relevant from the viewpoint of culture and identity. It reveals a lot about the poet and his background. He describes himself as 'a poet-rascal-clown' who grew up as a Jew among Christians, Muslims and Hindus in a state of suspicion and terror. As a boy, Ezekiel reports about his situation thus:

> I went to Roman Catholic school,
> A mugging Jew among the wolves.
> They told me I had killed the Christ,
> That year I won the scripture prize
> A Muslim sportsman boxed my ears.
> (*Ten Twentieth-Century Indian Poets*, 1976, 34-35)

Any Indian school, college, or university is a scene of mixed populace representing different religions, cultures and identities. Ezekiel's school in Bombay is merely an example of it. At the age of twenty-two, Ezekiel left for London where "Philosophy,/ Poverty and Poetry, three/ Companions shared my basement room" (*Ibid.*, 35). He could not make a headway there, and so he returned to India in exasperation. The poem is primarily autobiographical in content and form. He informs us about his ancestors as follows:

> The song of my experience sung.
> I knew that all was yet to sing.
> My ancestors, among the castes,
> Were aliens crushing seed for bread
> (The hooded bullock made his round).
> (1976, 36)

In the third section of the poem, Ezekiel tries to establish his cultural identity with the Indian landscape and Indian people, and says:

> I have made my commitments now,
> This is one: to stay where I am,
> ... ...

My backward place is where I am.
(1976, 37)

Besides this poem, Ezekiel tells us that "Scores of my poems are obviously written for personal, therapeutic purposes" (1976, 28). "Poet, Lover, Birdwatcher" is also a poem of this nature.

As for P. Lal, he gave a new direction, a new guideline, a new poetic manifesto to Indian English Poetry. His Kavita Manifesto was enunciated in 1958 when he along with K. Raghavendra Rao launched their anthology, *Modern Indo-Anglian Poetry.* The editors of this anthology divided Indian English poetry into two broad groups: the Aurobindonian and the non-Aurobindonian. The non-Aurobindonian is the modern or contemporary poetry. Credit goes to P. Lal and his Writers Workshop group to have infused a new lease of life, to have added a fresh approach and technique, to have initiated an imagistic and innovative idiom and expression, in Indian English Poetry. P. Lal makes a serious approach to love and life and sounds "a note of hope for man in this tension-ridden civilization" (*Indian Poetry in English: An Anthology*, 1980 & 1983, 119). Most of his poems are born of his experiences of love and beauty. One such poem is "Yakshi from Didarganj", which is steeped in love, romance and eroticism, reminding us of John Keats. A few lines from this poem are given below:

Bubbles of bead necklace like a river
Flow through the valley of her opulent breasts
Briefly trapping the touring eye; to their caver
These sandstone breasts with broken
Nipples were like apples taken
In token quenching of monumental thirst.
(Cited from *Indian Poetry in English Today*, ed. Pritish Nandy, 1973, 75-76)

This kind of sensuous and erotic poetry has been in the true tradition of Indian art, sculpture and paintings. The engravings in the caves of Ajanta and Ellora as well as on the hard stones of the Konark Temple are the glaring examples of it. P. Lal has done a great service to Indian poetry and religion by translating, nay by trans-creating, the complete *Mahabharata*.

Though it is not possible to catalogue the names of hundreds of Indian poets writing in English today, some of the outstanding ones may be mentioned here, such as Dom Moraes (1938-2004), A.K. Ramanujan (1929-93), Jayanta Mahapatra (1928-), Keki N. Daruwalla (1937-), A.K. Mehrotra (1947-), Kamala Das (1934-2008), Shiv K. Kumar (1921-2017), R. Parthasarathy (1934-), Keshav Malik (1924-2014), Pritish Nandy (1947-), Syed Amanuddin (1934-89), Syed Ameeruddin (1942-), Eunice de Souza (1940-), Smita Agarwal (1958-), Sujata Bhatt (1956-), Meena Alexander (1951-), and a few others. I must hasten to clarify that there are some others like Arun Kolatkar (1932-2004), Gieve Patel (1940-), Dilip Chitre (1938-2009) and O.P. Bhatnagar (1932-2001) who are also poetically gifted, and that I shall be arbitrarily selective in dealing with only a few of them, keeping in mind the constraints of time and space.

Dom Moraes has been a much-maligned and much-misunderstood poet. Ranjit Hoskote in his "Introduction" to *Dom Moraes' Selected Poems* considers Dom Moraes as a transcultural artist (2004 & 2012, lxxiii). He speculates that Moraes' poetry "would have been regarded as evidence of a postcolonial, even post-national, play of identities" (*Idem.*). Born to a Goan father and an East Indian mother and raised in an Anglophone ethos, he went to Oxford for higher education and started writing and publishing poems. Beginning with *A Beginning* (1957), he has published about eleven volumes of poetry to this day. His last volume was *Typed with One Finger* (2003). From the viewpoint of culture and identity, one particular poem, among many more, has captured my attention, and this poem is "Autobiography" which informs us about his grandmother—"crescent-browed,/ Falling from time, leaf-light, too much alone" (2004 & 2012, 11)—and his grandfather—"who was small and proud" (*Idem.*). The poem's last stanza deserves to be quoted in full as it throws light on the poet's life and craft:

> I have grown up, I think, to live alone
> To keep my old illusions, sometimes dream,
> Glumly, that I am unloved and forlorn.
> Run away from strangers, often seem
> Unreal to myself in the pulpy warmth of a sunbeam.

I have grown up, hand on the primal bone,
Making the poem, taking the word from the stream,
Fighting the sand for speech, fighting the stone.
(2004 & 2012, 12)

The poet's loneliness and frustration, his dreamy nature and sense of unreality, his lack of love and his composition of poetry: all are reflected here so beautifully.

A.K. Ramanujan is the finest flower of India's poetic genius. Despite his long stay in America, he never severed his associations with the land of his birth, with his family members and relations, with his friends and well-wishers. In his four volumes of poetry, from *The Striders* (1966) to *The Black Hen* (1995), Ramanujan has given us a number of poems steeped in Hindu myths and legends, gods and goddesses, rites and customs, religion and philosophy, culture and identity. Poems like "Snakes" and "A Hindu to his Body (in *The Strides),* "The Hindoo: he doesn't hurt a fly or a spider either, "The Hindoo: he reads his Gita and is calm at all events", "The Hindoo: the only risk" and "Prayers to Lord Murugun" (in *Relations*, 1971), "No Amnesiac King" (which is lesson-giving in nature), "A Minor Sacrifice", "Zoo Gardens Revisited", "Moulting" and "Second Sight" (in *Second Sight,* 1986), the three poems on Mythologies (in *The Black Hen,* 1995) are all of this kind. As an example of Ramanujan's culture and identity, we can quote "Zoo Gardens Revisited", especially the last lines:

Lord of lion face, boar snout, and fish eyes,
Killer of killer cranes, shepherd of rampant elephants,
Devour my lambs, devour them whole, save
them in the zoo garden ark of your belly.
(1986, 47)

Here various incarnations of Lord Vishnu as a protector have been alluded to. In "Moulting", a small prose poem, Garuda is invoked as the "Lord of snakes and eagles" (1986, 71). The three mythology poems refer unmistakably to the Krishna-Pootna episode, to the Vishnu-Hiranya Kashyapu tangle, and to the young female votary of Lord Shiva and her spouse story respectively. This is how Ramanujan writes in the first poem:

> The breast she offered was full
> of poison and milk.
> Flashing eyes suddenly dull,
> her voice was silk.
> The child took her breast
> in his mouth and sucked it right out of her chest.
> (1995, 221)

And in the third one he lets the female votary utter aloud to her loving groom thus:

> Keep off when I worship Shiva.
> Touch me three times, and you'll never
> see me again.... (1955, 228)

For the marvellous treatment of Hindu myths and legends, even folk-tales, A.K. Ramanujan has been considered to be "one of the most talented of the 'new' poets" (K.R.S. Iyengar, 1984 ed., 671). And Ramanujan resorts to it because it forms an essential ingredient of the "cultural determinant" of his imagination, as Chirantan Kulshrestha puts it (1978-79, 110).

From the viewpoint of culture and identity to be had in Contemporary Indian English Poetry, I have to limit my canvas of critical consideration, instead of recounting names of poets and their achievements. At the most, I am to consider briefly Keki N. Daruwalla and R. Parthasarathy among the male poets and Kamala Das, Sujata Bhatt and Smita Agarwal among the female poets (though I am fully aware that some other poets like Jayanta Mahapatra, A.K. Mehrotra, Pritish Nandy, Meena Alexander, Eunice de Souza, Imtiaz Dharker are quite inventive and thought-provoking).

Keki N. Daruwalla happens to be a powerful and provocative, also prolific, like Dom Moraes, poet of our times. In fact, he is a poet of 'rural landscape' of North India, just as Mahapatra is a forceful poet of Oriya landscape. In about a dozen poems, Daruwalla portrays the cultural identity of India, though he largely remains secular in his outlook upon life. The poems are: "We, the Kauravas" (*New Poems*, 2000-2005), "Shiva: At Timarsain" (*Under Orion*, 1970), "Pilgrimage to Badrinath" (*Apparition in April*, 1971) "Boat-ride Along the Ganga"

(*Crossing of Rivers*, 1976), "Aag-Matam" and "Sixth Moharram, Lucknow" (*The Keeper of the Dead*, 1982), "Agni Sutta", "The Birth of Maya", and "Draupadi" (*The Map-maker*, 2002). All these poems, taken together, clearly show that Daruwalla is a secular and open-minded person who has regards for all religions and ethical codes of life—for Hinduism, Buddhism, Islam, and Hebraism. I am tempted to quoted only two extracts from his poetry to prove my point of argument. One is taken from "Boat-ride along the Ganga", and runs as follows:

> Dante would have been confused here.
> Where would he place this city
> in Paradise or Purgatory, or lower down
> where fires smoulder beyond the reach of pity?
> The concept of the goddess baffles you—
> Ganga as mother, daughter, bride.
> What plane of destiny have I arrived at
> Where corpse-fires and cooking-fires
> burn side by side? (2006, 98)

This is a realistic portrayal of the city of Varanasi, especially of the burning ghat at Dashashwamedh, and the poet's tone has become ironic and sarcastic here, reminding us of the poetic style of Nissim Ezekiel. And the second extract is from "Aag-Matam" (i.e., "The Fire-mourning"), which depicts the agonising event of Imam Husain's tragic death. The last six lines of this poem are given below:

> Their thirst is a desert as they take the firewalk,
> their eyes are already on Karbala
> and heads that rolled and the babe Abdullah.
> Duldul, the faithful horse, frothing; the sword
> in Hussain's uplifted hand like a scythe
> and waiting for him the harvest of spears!
> (2006, 178-79)

And in "Agni Sutta", Daruwalla dwells on the Fire Sermon of Lord Buddha first delivered at Sarnath (not at Gaya, as the poet would make us believe), in a language which is at once evocative and incantatory.

Then I pass on to R. Parthasarathy, a poet of extremely austere style and terse diction. He has not written much, but his poetry is simply marvelous and sonorous. He began his poetic career with his poetical collection, *The First Step: Poems* 1956-66. Later he edited *Poetry from Leeds* (1968) in collaboration with J.J. Healey. He is, however, remembered today for his *Rough Passage* (1977), where he powerfully articulates the dilemma of a poet caught between two worlds, two tongues, two cultures, two identities. He writes thus:

> My tongue in English chains.
> I return, after a generation, to you.
> I am at the end
> of my dravidic tether,
> hunger for you unassuaged.
> I falter, stumble.
> Speak a tired language
> wrenched from its sleep in the *Kural*,
> teeth, palate, lip still new
> to its agglutinative touch.
> Now, hooked on celluloid, you reel
> down plush corridors. (1977, 44)

This is the shared experience of all bilingual poets, such poets as Arun Kolatkar, Dilip Chitre, Kamala Das, A.N. Dwivedi, and some others.

Kamala Das has been a confessional poet, following the trend started by Anne Sexton, Sylvia Plath, Robert Lowell (all Americans) and Judith Wright (Australian), and later practised by Gauri Deshpande and Meena Alexander (Indians). Kamala Das is the first Indian woman who has opted to write in English with candour and commitment, though her mother tongue is Malayalam. In her poem "An Introduction", she frankly writes thus:

> ... I am Indian, very brown, born in
> Malabar, I speak three languages, write in
> Two, dream in one. Don't write in English, they said
> English is not your mother-tongue.

... ...
The language I speak
Becomes mine, its distortions, its queernesses,
All mine, mine alone. It is half English, half
Indian, funny perhaps, but it is honest.
It is as human as I am human.... (1973, 27)

This passage reveals a good deal about the identity of Kamala Das, about her colour and birth, about her choice of language (-s), about her defence of the use of English as a mode of poetic utterance.

One remarkable characteristic of Indian women's poetry has been its integrity and honesty in articulating their age-long repressed desires, emotions and thoughts. Kamala Das took the lead; many others like Gauri Deshpande, Monika Varma, Meena Alexander, Eunice de Souza, Imtiaz Dharker, Sujata Bhatt, Melanie Silgardo, Tara Patel, Smita Agarwal, and Charmayne D'Souza followed her and strengthened this brand of poetry. Sujata Bhatt and Smita Agarwal are just lottery picks from the rich crop of women's poetry. Of the two, Sujata Bhatt has published four volumes of poetry, beginning with *Brunizem* (1988) which won the Commonwealth Poetry Prize for the Asia Region. Her *Monkey Shadows* (1991) was a Poetry Book Society Recommendation. What is striking about her poetry is its free and frank discussion of feminine longing, as in the poem "White Asparagus" (in *Monkey Shadows*) portraying the picture of a pregnant woman in her fourth month:

She is young, this is her first time,
She's slim and the nausea has gone.
Her belly's just starting to get rounder
her breasts itch all day,
and she's surprised that what she wants
is *him*
inside her again.
(*Nine Indian Women Poets*. 1997, 78)

The poet does not stop here, and invites her horseman for full sexual gratification:

> Oh come like a horse, she wants to say,
> move like a dog, a wolf,
> become a suckling lion-cub—
> Come here, and here, and here—
> but swim fast and don't stop. (*Ibid.*, 78-79)

The poem is highly erotic no doubt, but it also reveals the poet's delicate fancy and her feminine identity.

And last of all, Smita Agarwal is a fine poet of the new generation. Like Kamala Das and Sujata Bhatt, she treads on the familiar ground in her two volumes of poetry to date. Her first volume titled *Wish-Granting Words* (2002) contains a poem which focuses on man's unilateral decision (-s) affecting womankind. The poem is "Feb. 1944. Kasturba Talks of Life with Gandhi" where Gandhi has taken a sudden vow of celibacy in the pretext of his concentration, his assiduousness. Gandhi declares to his wife:

> Now, I'll live the life
> of a celibate. I'll feed and
> clothe you, and that's that....
> (*Wish-granting Words*, 2002, 24)

Hearing this one-sided decision, Kasturba becomes silent, as it is a denial of nature, of her natural instincts. More emotionally suffused poem is "Lopamudra" in her second volume, *Mofussil Notebook: Poems of Small-Town India* (2011), wherein she writes thus:

> Now, when I purr,
> Like a lioness in heat,
> you turn away....
> (2011, 76)

And he turns away at a time when "my breasts swell...the nipples itch/ And the two-little-fish-in-a-cow's-hoof-pond, throb" (*Ibid.*, 75). Smita's art touches the high watermark here. The artist in her is at full play in this poem. In a way, she is raising 'the woman question' in her own individualistic way.

IV

To conclude, in my survey of Contemporary Indian English Poetry, I have tried to be fair and brief. Of course, my approach is selective and arbitrary. Selection of a poet for discussion, or exclusion of a certain other, is a matter of choice or convenience. I have approached Indian English Poetry from the viewpoint of culture and identity. My overall impression of Contemporary Indian English Poetry is optimistic and positive, not negative and pessimistic as that of Uma Parameswaran, an Indian poet-cum-critic now based in Canada, who pronounced "the dirge-date" for Indian English Fiction as 2000 A.D. (1976, 6). As regards Indian English Poetry, I am of the view that it has become mature and solid enough to merit attention of the literary world, and that it will survive the scourge of unfavourable observations and circumstances in the days to come.

Works Cited

Agarwal, Smita. 2002. *Wish-Granting Words*. New Delhi: Ravi Dayal Publications Ltd.

———. 2011. *Mofussil Notebook: Poems of Small-Town India*. Cooperjal Ltd., UK: Ideaindia.com

Aurobindo, Sri. 1950-51. *Savitri*. Pondicherry: Sri Aurobindo Ashram.

———. 1972. *Collected Poems*. Pondicherry: Sri Aurobindo Ashram.

Bhabha, Homi K. 1994. *The Location of Culture*. London & New York: Routledge.

Bhatt, Sujata. 1997. "White Asparagus", *Nine Indian Women Poets*, ed. Eunice de Souza. New Delhi: O.U.P.

Daruwalla, Keki N. 2006. *Collected Poems*. New Delhi: Penguin Books India.

Das, Kamala. 1973. "An Introduction", *The Old Playhouse and Other Poems*. Madras: Orient Longman.

Dutt, Toru. 1882. *Ancient Ballads and Legends of Hindustan*. London: Kegan Paul & Co.

Dwivedi, A.N. 1979 & 1987. *Indo-Anglian Poetry*. Allahabad: Kitab Mahal.

———. 1980 & 1983. *Indian Poetry in English: An Anthology*. New Delhi: Arnold-Heinemann.

Ezekiel, Nissim. 1976. "Background, Casually" and "Poet, Lover, Birdwatcher", *Ten Twentieth-Century Indian Poets*. New Delhi: O.U.P.

Fanon, Frantz, 1961 & 2004. *The Wretched of the Earth*. New York: Grove Press.

Gosse, Sir Edmund. 1882. "Introductory Memoir", *Ancient Ballads and Legends of Hindustan* by Toru Dutt. London: Kegan Paul & Co.

Hall, Stuart & Paul du Gay. 1996 & 2008. *Questions of Cultural Identity*. Los Angeles & London: Sage Publications.

Iyengar, K.R. Srinivasa. 1962 & 1973; 4th ed. 1984. *Indian Writing in English*. New Delhi: Sterling Publishers Pvt. Ltd.

———. 1961. *Sri Aurobindo: An Introduction*. Mysore: Rao & Raghavan.

Kulshrestha, Chirantan. 1978-79. "The Self in Ramanujan's Poetry", *The Indian Journal of English Studies,* XVIII, 110-16.

Lal, P. & K. Raghvendra Rao. 1958. Eds. *Modern Indo-Anglian Poetry.* Calcutta: Writers Workshop.

Mishra, Pankaj. 2006. *Temptations of the West*. London: Picador.

Mongia, Padmini. 1996. Ed. *Contemporary Postcolonial Theory*. New Delhi: O.U.P.

Moraes, Dom. 2004 & 2012. *Dom Moraes: Selected Poems,* ed. Ranjit Hoskote, New Delhi: Penguin Books India.

Nandy, Pritish. 1973. Ed. *Indian Poetry in English Today*. New Delhi: Sterling Publishers Pvt. Ltd.

Parameswaran, Uma. 1976. *A Study of Representative Indo-English Novelists*. New Delhi: Vikas Publishing House.

Parthasarathy, R. 1977. *Rough Passage*. New Delhi: O.U.P.

———. 1976. Ed. *Ten Twentieth-Century Indian Poets*. New Delhi: O.U.P.

Ramanujan, A.K. 1986. *Second Sight*. New Delhi: O.U.P.

———. 1995. *The Black Hen in Collected Poems*. New Delhi: O.U.P.

Tagore, Rabindranath. 1913; 1973. *Gitanjali*. Madras: Macmillan Co. of India.

Yeats, W.B. 1913; 1973. "Introduction", *Gitanjali*. Madras: Macmillan Co. of India.

10

Changing Paradigms of Culture and Literature

Culture and literature are the two broad areas which have undergone tremendous change in the recent past. They are, in fact, interrelated. A literary man is usually regarded as a cultured man. When we think of culture and literature undergoing or having undergone change, we may allow them to be dynamic and volatile, not fixed and static. Scholars of cultural studies are of the general view that culture does not remain today monoculture because it has transcended the national boundaries and become transnational and transcultural. In other words, culture has now become globalized and hybridised. Similarly, literature has broadened its horizon to accommodate new trends and techniques, fresh ideas and philosophies, innovative researches and experiments in linguistic and literary theories. In points of culture and literature, the East and the West have drawn closer today than even before. I shall dwell, in my paper here, on some of the emerging trends and tendencies of culture and literature today.

Let us begin with a consideration of culture. In his well-known book, *The Wretched of the Earth* (1961), Frantz Fanon speaks about 'National Consciousness' and 'National Culture' in two separate chapters. Fanon thinks that the colonized people will have to play a crucial role in throwing out the colonizers (who invariably happen to be the imperialist powers of Europe) for elimination of such inequities as "forced labor, corporal punishment, unequal wages, and the restriction of political rights"

(1961 & 2004: 97). For arousing 'national consciousness', Fanon believes that the people's innermost aspirations must be stirred. And on the question of 'national culture', Fanon opines:

> In a colonized country, nationalism in its most basic, most rudimentary, and undifferentiated form is the most forceful and effective way of defending national culture. A culture is first and foremost the expression of a nation, its preferences, its taboos, its models. (*Ibid.*: 177)

Frantz Fanon is evidently concerned here with the traits of colonization and how national culture is helpful in getting rid of it in an effective way.

Culture is generally defined as "the beliefs, way of life, art, and customs that are shared and accepted by people in a particular society" (*Longman Dict.*, 1978 & 2003: 382). T.S. Eliot believes that religion, tradition and society are the pillars of culture. Matthew Arnold is of the view that the opposite of 'culture' is 'anarchy.' Some of the exponents of cultural studies are: Roland Barthes (who published *Mythologies* in 1957, trans. 1972), Raymond Williams (whose *Culture and Society* appeared in 1958), and Richard Hoggart (who wrote *The Uses of Literacy* in 1958, reprinted 1992). In the United States, the vogue for cultural studies had its roots mainly in 'the new historicism'. According to M.H. Abrams, its antecedents were both post-structural theorists like Louis Althusser and Michel Foucault and cultural anthropologists like Clifford Geertz (M.H. Abrams, 7th ed., 1999 & 2006: 53). The overall purpose of cultural studies is to subvert or negate the sharp distinction in traditional criticism between 'high literature' or 'high art' and 'lower forms' of literature or art that attract a much larger body of consumers. Cultural studies are devoted to popular fiction, romances (love stories), journalism and advertisement as well as to cartoon comics, film, television 'soap operas', and rock and rap music.

In the present-day scenario, culture has become transnational and transcultural. The noted critic, Homi K. Bhabha, calls it 'global cosmopolitanism'. In his illuminating book, *The Location of Culture* (1994 & 2007), Bhabha writes as follows:

> There is a kind of global cosmopolitanism, widely influential now, that configures the planet as a concentric world of national societies extending to global villages. It is a cosmopolitanism of relative prosperity and privilege founded on ideas of progress that are complicit with new-liberal forms of governance, and free market-forces of competition. Such a concept of global 'development' has faith in the virtually boundless powers of technological innovation and global communications. ("Introduction", xiv)

Bhabha aptly remarks that this kind of "global cosmopolitanism", which is identical to "globalization of national cultures", is linked with "imagined communities" consisting of "silicon valleys and software campuses", and that it "celebrates a world of plural cultures and peoples located at the periphery, so long as they produce healthy profit margins within metropolitan societies" (*Ibid.*). Bhabha is evidently hinting here at the confusion created by trans-culturalism or pluculturalism or multiculturalism. Bhabha hastens to add further that "Globalization must always begin at home" (xv).

Like Bhabha, scholars like Pnina Werbner and Tariq Modood focus their attention on 'cultural hybridity' and are concerned with the question of multi-cultural identities in their edited book, *Debating Cultural Hybridity* (London & New Jersey, 1997). As we know, the term 'hybridity' has been popularised by Homi Bhabha in the context of culture.

As for literature, it can be seen as a cultural construct along with education. Jonathan Culler, in this connection, remarks thus: "In principle, then, cultural studies includes and encompasses literary studies, examining literature as a particular cultural practice" (1997 & 2000: 43). Culler in his book, *Literary Theory: A Very Short Introduction* (1997 & 2000), suggests that it is "the literariness of texts of all sorts" that matters in literature, and that it is this literariness which distinguishes a literary work from a non-literary work. Culler further suggests as under:

> To reflect on literariness is to keep before us... reading practices elicited by literature: the

> suspension of the demand for immediate intelligibility, reflection on the implication of means of expression, and attention to how meaning is made and pleasure produced. (*Ibid.*: 41)

Jonathan Culler deals with 'the nature of literature' at some length and recounts the five points theorists have made about it. These five points are: 1. Literature as the 'foregrounding' of language; 2. Literature as the integration of language; 3. Literature as fiction; 4. Literature as aesthetic object; and 5. Literature as intertextual or self-reflective construct (*Ibid.*: 28-34). For one thing, Culler, like Benedict Anderson, underlines the value of the work of literature, particularly novels, which help create imagined national communities. Anderson writes, "Fiction seeps quietly and continuously into reality, creating that remarkable confidence of community in anonymity which is the hallmark of modern nations" (Cited from Culler: 37). The element of universality, which inspires the people to emulate the imagined community is, however, found not only in fiction but also in poetry, plays and other forms of writing.

In the Western context, literature is as old as two thousand five hundred years. Homer and Greek tragedians are the oldest surviving models of literature. In Indian history, the two great Sanskrit epics—the *Ramayana* and the *Mahabharata*—are the oldest extant literary works of immense value and power, putting aside the *Vedas*, *Upanishads* and *Puranas* as the scriptural texts. Since the times of the golden past, the human world has witnessed the rise and fall of currents and cross-currents of literature—of Classicism *vs.* Romanticism, of Tragedy *vs.* Comedy, of Pessimism *vs.* Optimism, etc.

Of late, literature has undergone a tremendous transformation. Lord Tennyson's famous dictum "The old order changeth yielding place to new" is precisely applicable to modern literature (which roughly begins with the first quarter of the 20th century). Modernism is set in motion in English literature after the First World War (1914-18). The year 1922 saw the publication of a few monumental works like James Joyce's *Ulysses*, Virginia Woolf's *Jacob's Room*, and T.S. Eliot's *The Waste Land*. William Butler Yeats, Ezra Pound, Gertrude Stein, Marcel Proust, Andrè Gide,

Franz Kafka, William Faulkner, William Carlos Williams, Wallace Stevens, and many others joined the bandwagon of Modernism. These modernists tried to subvert, according to M.H. Abrams, "the basic conventions of earlier prose fiction [even earlier poetry-*mine*] by breaking up the narrative continuity, departing from the standard ways of representing characters, and violating the traditional syntax and coherence of narrative language by the use of stream of consciousness and other innovative modes of narration" (1999 & 2006: 167). In the domain of poetry, T.S. Eliot blows the bugle of revolt against the traditional poetry. To elaborate the point, one can compare the opening of *The Waste Land* and that of Chaucer's Prologue to the *Canterbury Tales* and mark the sheer contrast in them.

Postmodernism in literature and fine arts is both a continuation of "the countertraditional experiments of modernism" and also a departure from the modernist form of expression by overthrowing "the elitism of modernist 'high art' by recourse to the models of 'mass culture' in film, television, newspaper cartoons, and popular music" (Abrams: 168). Postmodernism arose in the 1970s with the publication of Jean-Francois Lyotard's *La Condition Postmoderne* (1978; English version, 1984) and Jean Baudrillard's *Simulations* (1981; English translation, 1983). In *The Postmodern Condition*, Lyotard raises his objections to the contemporary German theorist Jurgen Habermas's postulations that a major moment in the history of Postmodernism is the rise of the Enlightenment or the Age of Reason (the period of one hundred years from the mid-seventeenth to the mid-eighteenth century), with its insistence on reason, purpose, coherence and order. Toeing the line of Habermas, Niall Lucy in his book *Postmodern Literary Theory* pleads for 'the Return of Reason' in the postmodern age (1997 & 2002: 247-49). Lyotard, however, believes that the postmodern age is characterized by lack of centrality and certainty, by loss of a sense of history and disbelief in the triumph of science (which, in fact, generate Lyotard's suspicion of 'metanarratives'), and as such it cannot be a revival of the Age of Reason. According to Linda Hutcheon, postmodernism appears before us in various shades and colours: "For some it was a mere 'moment', while for others it was a more general 'condition'. Some denigrated it to just a 'style'; still others elevated it to a historical 'period'" (2006: 115). Christopher Butler thinks that postmodernism has though created 'electronic means' of communication, it is "not particularly unified in doctrine" and it is "certain of its uncertainty" (2002: 2-3). Some of the well-known postmodernist writers are Samuel Becket, Jorge Luis Borges, Vladimir Nabokov, Thomas Pynchon, Roland Barthes, Salman Rushdie and Amitav Ghosh.

The theory of Colonialism/Postcolonialism (see Ania Loomba's book, 1998) is clearly linked to historical and political events affecting mankind. The imperial powers of Europe—England, Spain, France, Portugal, etc.—were spurred with ambition to expand their power and trade in other countries. Their superior arms and military strength enabled them to win other countries and make them their colonies. To keep such other countries under their governance, the imperialists appointed governors, governor-generals or viceroys through whom they imposed their language and culture on subject-nations. Michel Foucault calls this process 'cultural imperialism'. Under this mode of imperialism, the European powers made their own language and culture an integral part of the educational system of the colonized countries. In the Indian context, Macaulay's *Minute* proved epoch-making in imposing English as the medium of instruction in schools, colleges and universities. More or less, the same situation prevailed in West Indies, South Africa, Nigeria, Kenya, Sri Lanka, Pakistan, and some other countries of Asia, Africa and the Caribbean. When these countries became free one by one, they revolted against the master's language and culture. We can have a glimpse of it in Caliban's revolt against Prospero in William Shakespeare's *The Tempest* (1910-11). Edward Said's *Orientalism* (1978), which considered the construction of the Oriental 'other' by European discourses of knowledge, marks the beginning of postcolonial theory. The critical text of Edward Said assumes that everything 'occidental' is pre-eminent and superior, while everything 'oriental' is exotic and inferior. The oriental other' or 'the colonial other' is "not only subordinated and marginalized but in effect deleted as a cultural agency" (Abrams, 1999 & 2006: 236-37). After independence of the erstwhile colonized countries, including India, the process of decolonization started, and the authors/cultures of these countries began re-writing their history with a sense of self-assertion. This point is so well raised in *The Empire Writes Back: Theory and Practice in Post-colonial Literatures* (1989), edited by Bill Ashcroft, Gareth Griffiths and Helen Tiffin.

One direct result of the postcolonial agenda is to destabilize "Eurocentric norms of literary and artistic values", and to expand "the literary canon to include colonial and postcolonial writers" (Abrams: 237). Margaret Drabble in her edited book, *The Oxford Companion to English Literature* (6th ed. 2000, rev. 2006), acknowledges the significance of the new literatures in English constituting "a body of exciting and dynamic texts capable at once of forcing a reassessment of the traditional canon and of providing a vigorous alternative to what are often regarded as rather defensive and introspective English texts" (809). This changed attitude is responsible for revival of interest in the writings of several postcolonial authors—Anita Desai, Salman Rushdie, Amitav Ghosh, Arundhati Roy, Aravind Adiga among the Indians; V.S. Naipaul and Derek Walcott among the Caribbeans; Chinua Achebe, Wole Soyinka and Ngugi wa Thiong'o among the Africans.

Since the postcolonial theory highlights the plight of 'the other'—the poor and the downtrodden, the oppressed and the exploited—it gives its thought to the question of 'the subaltern'. Gayatri Chakravorty Spivak in her lengthy essay "Can the Subaltern Speak?" (1988), later reprinted in *The Postcolonial Studies Reader* (1995), eds. Bill Ashcroft, Gareth Griffiths, and Helen Tiffin, pleads for the voice of the so-long voiceless subalterns about themselves. The subalterns include the deprived and destitute class, negroes, Blacks, Dalits and SCs and STs (in the Indian context), as well as the womankind. All these classes of people, including women, have now become vocal in literature.

We know, women writers have created a special brand of literature today which is usually called 'feminist' literature. They claim to follow a path different from that of male writers; as against the 'phallocentric' male writers, they remain 'gynocentric'. Elaine Showalter in her book, *A Literature of Their Own* (1977), pleads for 'gynocriticism' in literature which lays down "a specifically female framework for dealing with works written by women... (Abrams: 91). The foundation of such an assertion was laid by a number of feminist thinkers and scholars, such as Mary Wollstonecraft (*A Vindication of the Rights of Women*, 1792), John Stuart Mill (*The Subjection of Women*, 1969), Margaret Fuller (*Woman in the Nineteenth Century*, 1845), Virginia Woolf (*A Room of One's Own,* 1929), Simone de Beauvoir (*The Second Sex*, 1949), Mary Ellmanemech (*Thinking about Women*, 1968), and Kate Millett (*Sexual Politics,* 1969). The last-named author uses the term 'politics' to signify "the mechanisms that express and enforce the relations of power in society" (Abrams: 88). She attacks the male bias in Freud's pyscho-analytic theory and also analyses selected passages by D.H. Lawrence, Henry Miller, Norman Mailer, and Jean Genet to show male aggrandisement and female degradation as submissive sexual objects. The impact of these feminist thinkers and scholars has been immense and hundreds of women writers have come up on the literary horizon of the world. In India itself, we have a host of women writers like Kamala Markandaya, Anita Desai, Shashi Deshpande, Nayantara Sahgal, Shobha De, Arundhati Roy, Kiran Desai, Githa Hariharan and Gita Mehta among the novelists, and Toru Dutt, Sarojini Naidu, Kamala Das, Lila Ray, Monika Varma, Eunice d'Souza, Sujata Bhatt, Lakshmi Kannan, and Meena Alexander among the poets. They are all writing about women and their issues in a forceful manner.

Last of all, I have to take up the theory of Deconstruction expounded by the French thinker Jacques Derrida. Deconstruction is not so much "a mode of literary criticism" as "a way of reading all kinds of texts so as to reveal and subvert the tacit metaphysical pre-suppositions of Western thought" (Abrams: 59). According to Margaret Drabble, it is "an approach to the reading of literary and philosophical texts that casts doubt upon the possibility of finding in them a definitive meaning, and that traces instead the multiplication (or 'dissemination') of possible meanings" (2006 rev. ed.: 265). Thus, a deconstructive reading of a poem will not end with the discovery of its essential meaning, but with an impasse or deadlock or 'double bind' ('aporia'). Jonathan

Culler observes that "Deconstruction is most simply defined as a critique of the hierarchical oppositions that have structured Western thought: Inside/outside, mind/body, literal/metaphorical, speech/writing, presence/absence, nature/culture, form/meaning" (1997 & 2000: 126). Derrida calls them 'binary oppositions', which do not allow a fixed meaning to texts. The 'differance' of binary oppositions keeps the meaning fluid and unstable. Derrida presents his basic views in three books, all published in 1967, which are entitled *Of Grammatology, Writing and Difference,* and *Speech and Phenomena.* Later, his American followers at Yale and elsewhere, such as Paul de Man, Barbara Johnson, and J. Hillis Miller popularized deconstructive readings through their works. They are agreed on the point that 'deconstruction' is not synonymous with 'destruction', and that it is a "careful teasing out of warring forces of signification within the text itself" (Barbara Johnson). It is not a dismantling of the structure of a text but 'a demonstration that it has already dismantled itself' (J.H. Miller). It is, thus, close to poststructuralist's approach to language. Its 'close reading' of a text draws it nearer to 'critical analysis' of a text in New Criticism. Jonathan Culler holds the view that "contemporary feminisms, psychoanalytic theories, Marxisms and historicisms, all partake in post-structuralism", and that "*post-structuralism* also designates...*deconstruction* and the work of Jacques Derrida" (1997 & 2000: 125-26).

To conclude, I have discussed above the changing paradigms of culture and literature and have tried to show that they are dynamic and changeable. No literature is possible without language and no culture is thinkable without literature. Hence, they are closely connected to each other. They are open to new trends and tendencies, and as such are situationally alive and accommodative in nature.

Works Cited

Abrams, M.H. 1999 & 2006. *A Glossary of Literary Terms*. India ed. New Delhi: Thomson Heinle.

Anderson, Benedict. 1983 & 2006. *Imagined Communities*. London & New York: Verso.

Ashcroft, Bill, Gareth Griffiths and Helen Tiffin. 1989. *The Empire Writes Back*. London & New York: Routledge.

Bhabha, Homi K. 1994. *The Location of Culture*. London & New York: Routledge.

Butler, Christopher. 2002. *Postmodernism: A Very Short Introduction.* Oxford: O.U.P.

Culler, Jonathan. 1997 & 2000. *Literary Theory: A Very Short Introduction*. Oxford: O.U.P.

Drabble, Margaret, 6th ed. 2000, rev. 2006. *The Oxford Companion to English Literature.* Oxford: O.U.P.

11

Nation, Culture and Identity: Theory and Texts in the 21st Century*

In this age of globalization, the national boundaries are collapsing. While globalization is usually a gift of the West, national identity is the concern of the race, community, religion and culture belonging to that nation. It is possible that a country like India, South Africa, the United Kingdom or the United States has to confront the problem of subversion and destabilization due to the presence of multiple communities, creeds and colours, and then the national integrity is sometimes threatened by internal as well as external forces. But it is only a hypothesis. The thesis is that the greater the challenges or threats, the stronger is the response of an alert nation and its citizens. Israel is a glaring example of it. That calls for a strong patriotic perception towards the nation-state on the part of its citizens in an otherwise fast-changing global scenario where the problem of national or cultural identity remains in a 'fluid' or 'liquid' condition, as the famous sociologist Zygmunt Bauman also thinks (2004: 89).

I

A nation, in political terms, is defined as "large number of people of mainly common descent, language, history, etc., usually inhabiting a territory bounded by defined limits and forming a society under one government" (*C.O.D.*, 1911, 6th ed. 1975: 725). There are also other definitions, such as those

* Keynote Address delivered at the national seminar held at Pt. Sundarlal Sharma Open University, Bilaspur (Chhattisgarh) on February 11, 2017.

of Benedict Anderson, Joseph Stalin, and Bipin Chandra Pal. Of these thinkers, Anderson considers nation as an "imagined community" (*Imagined Communities: Reflections on the Origin and Spread of Nationalism*, 1991 & 2006: 6-7). By 'imagined communities' Anderson means 'those living in the silicon valley' (as Bill Ashcroft *et al.* would express it) or those moving in the cosmopolitan world (as Homi Bhabha would put it). Anderson argues that "nationness is the most universally legitimate value in the political life of our times" (1991 & 2006: 3). Anderson further argues that the birth of nationalism in Western Europe is co-existent with the dwindling of religious modes of thought. The rationalist secularism of the Enlightenment (that took place in the second half of the 18th century, precisely in 1774 A.D.) was mainly responsible for the devastation of old religious systems and sociality. Anderson is of the view that nationalism fills up the existential void created by the loss of existence, and that the nation is, thus, the product of a radically secular and modern imagination. Anderson though talks of 'imagined communities' and 'a radically secular and modern imagination', he does not think of 'nation' as something imaginary or fictious. He rather links the inevitability of the modern nation-state with the successive progression of human history. Stalin thinks that "A nation is primarily a community, a definite community of people" and that "a nation is not a racial or tribal but a historically constituted community of people" (*Marxism and the National Question*, cited from *Works*, Vol. 2, 1954: 300-81). And Bipin Chandra Pal, a great nationalist leader of India, observes that "There is a very wide difference between a race and a nation. In the first place, territorial unity is an essential condition of nationality, but not of raciality. A race may spread over different and distant territories, and occupy various parts of the globe, but a nation must be confined to a definite habitat" (*Nationality and Empire*, 1916, LPP ed. 2002: 3). While Stalin links nation with history, Pal connects it to territorial unity or geographical entity.

At the present moment, the concept of nation is undergoing a significant transformation. The process of globalization has set in the era of transnationalism and transculturalism, and it is instrumental in breaking asunder national boundaries. The concept of transnationalism has stepped in to disturb the concept of nationalism, the concept of centrality. It poses a challenge to the forces of the nation-state, and envisages "a crossing of national borders, a cultural/political interplay between different national cultures, or a mode of mobility of transnational subjects" (Joel Kuortti & Om Prakash Dwivedi: *Changing Worlds Changing Nations: The Concept of a Nation in the Transnational Era,* 2012: 2). In other words, transnationalism is a kind of multinationalism; it is something that shares cultural connections with more than one nation. The dualism of the nation-state is best articulated in Robert Frost's poem "Mending Wall" where the speaker first says:

> Something there is that doesn't love a wall,
> That sends the frozen-ground-swell under it,
> And spills the upper boulders in the sun;
> And makes gaps even two can pass abreast.
> The work of hunters is another thing.
>
> (*The Pocket Book of Modern Verse,* 1954 & 1967: 235)

But later in the poem, the speaker-persona recalls his father's saying and observes: "Good fences make good neighbors" (236). Fences are evidently needed for the individual nation-states, not for those believing in an international co-existence or in a world-order.

Frantz Fanon in his famous book, *The Wretched of the Earth* (1961), devotes two lengthy chapters on "The Trials and Tribulations of National Consciousness" and "On National Culture" respectively and through his enlightening arguments stimulates us to think of the crucial role of the people (who were once colonized) in waging a war against the colonizers for elimination of iniquities such as "forced labor, corporal punishment, unequal wages, and the restriction of political rights" (97). For national consciousness, according to Fanon, it is necessary to awaken 'the people's innermost aspirations'. For achieving national independence, as eventually America, India, South Africa and some other countries did, the national bourgeoisie must be stirred to action, even to fight to take over "power at the end of the colonial regime" (98). Another valid point raised by Fanon in his book is that merely national independence is not enough, it must be accompanied with economic self-reliance. Fanon rightly suggests that the national parties usually do not have "a clue about the economy of their own country" (99), and this adds to the trials and tribulations of national consciousness. On the question of 'national culture', Fanon is of the view:

> In a colonized country, nationalism in its most basic, most rudimentary, and undifferentiated form is the most forceful and effective way of defending national culture. A culture is first and foremost the expression of a nation, its preferences, its taboos, its models. (1961 & 2004: 177)

A little onward, Fanon further opines that "the conscious, organized struggle undertaken by a colonized people in order to restore national sovereignty constitutes the greatest cultural manifestation..." (178). A nation can have a tongue, a literature, a culture, a set boundary of its own. A new literature often springs from the birth of a new nation.

The first postcolonial society to develop a 'national' literature was the USA, followed by India, Pakistan, Sri Lanka, South Africa, and Australia (to name only a few countries). National literature is a by-product of the social and political history of a country. Its customs, rituals, thoughts, and beliefs feed and sustain national literature. For India, Hindi is our national language. And Hindi gets sustained by the rich vocabulary and the sound grammar of Sanskrit. But English in India plays the role of a link language, a language of communication between the Centre and the States as well as between States themselves. Bill Ashcroft, Gareth Griffiths and Helen Tiffin have drawn our attention to national and regional models of new (or postcolonial) literature in their learned book, *The Empire Writes Back* (1989: 15-17).

There is yet another aspect of the nationalist discourse, and that is related to the assumption that some nations are 'good' and progressive, while others are 'bad' and reactionary. In her illuminating book, *Postcolonial Theory: A Critical Introduction* (1998: 103-10), Leela Gandhi deals with this kind of chronic distinction between 'good' and 'bad', or 'legitimate' and 'illegitimate', nationalisms.

As for culture, it has a wide variety of connotations. So long we were talking about nation and national culture, but in its vaster application it may become international culture or transnational culture. *Longman Dictionary of Contemporary English* (1978 & 2003: 382) clearly hints at its variety, hybridity and complexity when it attempts to define it in the context of a society, a group, a nation, or in relation to art, music and literature. It jots down about culture thus: "the beliefs, way of life, art, and customs that are shared and accepted by people in the particular society" (382).

The study of culture inevitably draws us close to what M.H. Abrams calls "a recent and rapidly growing cross-disciplinary enterprise for analyzing the conditions that effect the production, reception and cultural significance of all types of institutions, practices, and products..." (*A Glossary of Literary Terms*, 7th ed., 1999 & 2006: 53). Literature is one of cultural practices. Some of the exponents of cultural studies are: Roland Barthes (who wrote *Mythologies*, 1957, trans. 1972), Raymond Williams (who published *Culture and Society*, 1958), and Richard Hoggart (who brought out *The Uses of Literacy*, 1958, reprinted 1992). Their efforts bore fruits when it became institutionalized in the influential Birmingham Centre for Contemporary Cultural Studies (founded by Hoggart in 1964). Across the Atlantic in the United States, the vogue for cultural studies had its roots mainly in the mode of literary and cultural criticism known as 'the new historicism'. According to M.H. Abrams, its antecedents were both poststructural theorists like Louis Althusser and Michel Foucault and cultural anthropologists like Clifford Geertz (*A Glossary of Literary Terms,* 53). The overall purpose of cultural studies is to subvert or negate the sharp distinction in traditional criticism between 'high literature' and 'high art' and 'lower forms' of literature and art that attract a much larger body of consumers. Cultural studies pay greater attention to popular fiction, romances (love stories), journalism and advertising as well as to arts of popular appeal such as cartoon comics, film, television 'soap operas', and rock and rap music, as M.H. Abrams further suggests (53).

Culture has its opponent in 'anarchy', as Matthew Arnold hinted at in the Victorian age in his famous book, *Culture and*

Anarchy (1967-68). Arnold's contention is that culture has to contend with philistinism (a term used for 'lack of culture') and Americanism (a term signifying 'meanness of spirit'). Obviously, when culture is threatened, great qualities of head and heart are trodden down and 'littleness united' becomes 'invincible', and Arnold subscribes to this view.

Even today, culture is facing a good deal of challenges. Now culture has become transnational and transcultural. Homi K. Bhabha calls it 'global cosmopolitanism'. Writing about it in his bright book, *The Location of Culture* (London & New York: Routledge, 1994; Indian rpt. 2007: xiv-xv), Bhabha points out:

> There is a kind of global cosmopolitanism, widely influential now, that configures the planet as a concentric world of national societies extending to global villages. It is a cosmopolitanism of relative prosperity and privilege founded on ideas of progress that are complicit with neo-liberal forms of governance, and free market-forces of competition. Such a concept of global 'development' has faith in the virtually boundless powers of technological innovation and global communications. (xiv)

Bhabha rightly suggests that this sort of 'global cosmopolitanism' (which is the same as 'globalization of national culture') celebrates "a world of plural cultures and peoples located at the periphery so long as they produce healthy profit margins within metropolitan societies". Bhabha adds further: "States that participate in such multicultural multinationalism affirm their commitment to 'diversity', at home and abroad, so long as the demography of diversity consists largely of educated economic migrants—computer engineers, medical technicians, and entrepreneurs, rather than refugees, political exiles, or the poor" (*Ibid.*, xiv). Bhabha is hinting here at the confusion created by transculturalism or pluculturalism or multinational culturalism. Bhabha emphatically states that "Globalization must always begin at home", and that "a just measure of global progress requires that we first evaluate how globalizing nations deal with the difference within"... (xv).

Like Bhabha, Pt. Jawaharlal Nehru speaks of cultural diversity in India. He acknowledges the existence of different races, ethnic groups, social customs and practices, languages, castes, colours and creeds in India, and eventually evolves the formula of 'unity in diversity' in his monumental work, *The Discovery of India* (1946). He even suggests that India is a sub-continent, rather a mini world. Scholars like Pnina Werbner and Tariq Modood focus their debate on 'cultural hybridity' and are concerned with the question of multi-cultural identities in their edited book, *Debating Cultural Hybridity* (London & New Jersey: Zed Books, 1997).

Evidently, one is readily recognised by one's nation and culture, but the problem of recognition deepens when one crosses the boundaries of race, society, nation, community, language and culture. Once T.S. Eliot was asked as to why he gave up the study of Sanskrit and Pali, and he answered that he was not prepared to relinquish his identity as an American or later as a European (see his *After Strange Gods*, 1934).

Scholars like Stuart Hall and Paul du Gay raise the questions of cultural identity in their edited book, *Questions of Cultural Identity* (Los Angeles & London: Sage Publications, 1996 & 2008), in an emphatic way and veer round the idea that identity is 'the formation of subjectivity[1] ("Introduction", 9). Identity is akin to a sense of 'belonging'. In his insightful paper, Stuart Hall thinks that the question of identity operates within the ambit of relationship of the 'self' to 'the other'. He brackets 'identity' with 'identification' (*Ibid.*, 2), and opines that the theorization of identity is "a matter of considerable political significance" (*Ibid.*, 16). Even Derrida (See his *Positions*. Chicago: Univ. of Chicago Press, 1981) has shown that an identity's constitution is based on excluding something and establishing a violent hierarchy between the two resultant poles—man/woman, etc. Derrida postulates the theory of 'binary opposition' (e.g., day/night; white/black; rich/poor, etc.) in order to determine the question of identity.

II

We have already observed the theoretical postulations of terms like nation, culture and identity. Now is the turn of a critical-cum-analytical study of a few works of fiction, not many, of course, in the light of the theories outlined in the foregoing pages.

Since the publication of Salman Rushdie's *Midnight's Children* in 1981, it has become customary to bring out a text as an admixture of the history of a nation and the history of an individual. Rushdie admirably combines the two in a rare feat of artistic achievement when he writes at the beginning of his epoch-making novel:

> I [Saleem Sinai] was born in the city of Bombay—once upon a time. No, that won't do, there is no getting away from the date: I was born in Doctor Narlikar's Nursing Home on August 15th, 1947. And the time: the time matters, too, Well then, at night. No, it is important to be more.... On the stroke of midnight, as a matter of fact. Oh, spell it out, spell it out: at the precise instant of India's arrival at independence, I tumbled forth into the world.... I had been mysteriously handcuffed to history, my destinies indissolubly chained to those of my country. (*Midnight's Children*, 1981 & 1995: 2)

As a postmodernist text dealing with the birth of a nation, history is presented here in a fragmented form—one vast sub-continent is broken into two free nations. It is a kind of disfiguration of history or a dehistoricization of history. In this novel, the boundaries of nation-state are in a state of flux, are deconstructed and then reconstructed. Here the personal history of Saleem Sinai is merged into the national history and *vice versa*. In this novel, characters live and act and events shape in a world of make-believe, in a world of magical realism. The stories of Saleem's grandfather (Aadam Aziz), his father, Tai, the boatman, and midnight's children unfold a wealth of unbelievable, almost super, powers and tricks.

Arundhati Roy's *The God of Small Things* (1997) is definitely a very popular novel wherein so many literary theories have been put in place, such as poststructuralism, feminism, postcolonialism, and postmodernism. Hans Bertens, who wrote *The Idea of the Post-modern* (1995), comments in another critical book titled *Literary Theory: The Basics* (2001) that the postmodernist writing "unsettles and deconstructs traditional notions about language, about identity, about writing itself, and so on" (141). In Roy's novel, we come across a good deal of experiments about language and identity. She employs lively words, phrases and expressions in her fictional work; for example; "He [the one-armed man] could do only one thing at a time. If he held her, he couldn't kiss her. If he kissed her, he couldn't see her. If he saw her, he could not feel her" (1997: 4). The identity of the one-armed man is shrouded in mystery till the very end. And equally intriguing is the spicy language, such as in the following: "The God of Loss/ The God of Small Things./ The God of Goose Bumps and Sudden Smiles" (5 & 330). The reader must mark the use of capital letters—unexpected and unwanted as they are—violating the rules of grammar/punctuation. Prof. C.D. Narasimhaiah finds fault with Roy's verbosity and excesses (see *The Literary Criterion*, Winter 1997: V), but Anna Sujatha Mathai approves of her practice: "Roy's sense of the language, her constant exploration and tasting, testing, balancing of it, adds to the originality and joy of the book" (*Indian Literature*, July-August 1997: 180). The novel also considers the question of identity in a prominent way by dwelling on the tragic life-story of Velutha, a subaltern, in a rigid Hindu society.

Two novels must be mentioned here as topical allusions to burning national problems, and they are: *The Lowland* (2013) by Jhumpa Lahiri and *The Lives of Others* (2014) by Neel Mukherjee. Both of them deal with the Naxalite movement raging in West Bengal during the late 1960s. Udayan, the younger brother of Subhas, spearheads the movement in Lahiri's novel, and Supratik Ghosh champions it in Mukherjee's work, and both the protagonists meet a tragic end at the hands of the government machinery or what you call police. The two novels remind us of the Partition novels wherein the sufferings and mutilations of the people, the pangs of the division of a nation, occupy the forefront and steal the limelight.

For a study of the cultural constructs, we can go to such latest novels as Aravind's *The White Tiger* (2008), Jeet Thayil's *Narcopolis* (2012) and Jerry Pinto's *Em and the Big Hoom* (2012). By naming these authors and texts, I don't mean that the list is exhausted. More authors and their texts can be definitely included in it. But the three authors and their texts mentioned here are enough to show the climax of 'high culture' and 'low culture'.

The novels by Adiga and Thayil show the decline of culture in the age of globalization and modernization. Adiga depicts the binary of master/servant relationship, the struggle of a subordinate/subaltern for money and power. In his autobiographical novel, Adiga portrays Balram Halwai, the son of a rickshaw-puller, becoming a driver for Mr. Ashok and his wife Madam Pinky. Reaching Delhi for some personal work, Mr. Ashok trusts the driver, who impelled by greed and ambition kills his master in a deserted place for "seven hundred thousand rupees" (2008: 281). With the money, Balram flees to the deep South, precisely to Bengaluru, in the company of his nephew Dharam. There Balram becomes "a business entrepreneur" (299) and attains success in it as a follower of the consumerist culture,—a culture that gives the city of Bengaluru its present identity.

Jeet Thayil depicts the 'low culture' of the dwellers of slums and the gutter in Old Bombay. His novel, *Narcopolis*, written in the style of De Quincey and Burroughs graphically captures Rashid, an opium-addict, in the terrible grip of the pipe (see Ch. 9: "The Pipe Comes to Rashid", pp. 123-32). Cast in four books, the novel shows Rashid and a woman holding a long-stemmed pipe over a flame as men sprawl and mutter in the gloom. In Shuklaji Street, Old Bombay, people say that one introduces only one's worst enemy to opium. Based on the author's experience of twenty years, the scintillating story of opium and heroin highlights the poor and miserable conditions of drug-addicts as represented by Rashid and Dimple (a street prostitute) living in a den.

But Jerry Pinto comes as a contrast to Adiga and Thayil. The novel, *Em and the Big Hoom*, is delightful, witty and humorous, and is woven around a family of four living in Mahim, Bombay. The mother called Imelda is shown fighting heroically with her mental illness, her ever-persisting depression, without letting her husband (called Augustine, also Mambo and Augie March) and children (son Baba and daughter Susan) feel the pinch of her sickness. The family shares the sorrows and joys of others in a jovial or serious mood. Me/Mother is a woman of taste, a singer of a sort, a lover of books. Sometimes she goes to bookshops because "they were civilized places" (2012: 101).

III

To conclude, I have explained above a few terms of literary theory like 'nation', 'culture' and 'identity' and tried to connect them with some well-known texts of our times. Though critics like Niall Lucy (in *Postmodern Literary Theory: An Introduction*, Oxford, Blackwell Publishers Inc., 1997), pronouncing the death of history, the death of criticism, and the death of theory (see Chs. 3, 6 & 9 for this; pp. 42-62; 104-21; & 163-83), and Peter Barry listing Books against Theory (pp. 329-30), and Roland Barthes declaring the Death of the Author, frighten us terribly in our pursuit of Literary Theory, we can march ahead with firm determination not to be deterred by them. For our goal is knowledge, and the search for knowledge is always fruitful and rewarding.

Works Cited

Abrams, M.H. 1999 & 2006. *A Glossary of Literary Terms*. India ed. New Delhi: Thomson/Heinle.

Adiga, Aravind. 2008. *The White Tiger*. Noida, London: HarperCollins Publishers.

Anderson, Benedict. 1983 & 2006. *Imagined Communities: Reflections on the Origin and Spread of Nationalism*. London & New York: Verso.

Arnold, Matthew. 1867-68. *Culture and Anarchy:* OUP.

Ashcroft, Bill, Gareth Griffiths and Helen Tiffin. 1989. *The Empire Writes Back*. London & New York: Routledge.

Bauman, Zygmunt. 2004. *Identity: Conversations with B. Vecchi*. Cambridge: Polity Press.

Bertens, Hans. 1995. *The Idea of the Postmodern*. London and New York: Routledge.

———. 2001. *Literary Theory: The Basics*. London: Psychology Press.

Bhabha, Homi K. 1994. *The Location of Culture*. London & New York: Routledge.

Concise Oxford Dictionary, The. 1911; 6th ed. 1975. Oxford: OUP.

Derrida, Jacques, 1981. *Positions. Chicago: Chicago University Press.*

Eliot, T.S. 1934. *After Strange Gods*. London: Faber & Faber.

Fanon, Frantz. 1961 & 2004. *The Wretched of the Earth*. New York: Grove Press.

Frost, Robert. 1954 & 1967. "Mending Wall", *The Pocket Book of Modern Verse*. New York: Washington Square Ltd., Inc.

Gandhi, Leela, 1998. *Postcolonial Theory: A Critical Introduction*. New Delhi: OUP.

Hall, Stuart & Paul du Gay. 1996 & 2008. Eds. *Questions of Cultural Identity*. Los Angeles & London: Sage Publications.

Kuortti, Joel and Om Prakash Dwivedi. 2012. Eds. *Changing Worlds Changing Nations: The Concept of a Nation in the Transnational Era*. Jaipur, New Delhi, etc.: Rawat Publications.

Lahiri, Jhumpa. 2013. *The Lowland*. Noida & London: Random House Publishers.

Longman Dictionary of Contemporary English. 1978 & 2003. Essex, England: Pearson Education Ltd.

Lucy, Niall. 1997. *Postmodern Literary Theory: An Introduction*. Oxford: Blackwell Publishing.

Mathai, Anna Sujatha. July-August 1997. *Indian Literature*, a Sahitya Akademi journal.

Mukherjee, Neel. 2014. *The Lives of Others*. London: Chatto & Windus.

Narasimhaiah, C.D. Winter 1997. "The Booker Prize: A Curse to Creativity", *The Literary Criterion*.

Nehru, Jawaharlal. 1946. *The Discovery of India*. Calcutta: The Signet Press.

Pal, Bipin Chandra. 1916; LPP ed. 2002. *Nationality and Empire*. New Delhi: L.P. Publications.

Pinto, Jerry. 2012. *Em and the Big Hoom*. New Delhi: Aleph Book Co.

Roy, Arundhati. 1997. *The God of Small Things*. New Delhi: IndiaInk.

Rushdie, Salman. 1981 & 1995. *Midnight's Children*. London, U.K.: Jonathan Cape Ltd.

———. 2008. *The Enchantress of Florence*. London, U.K: Jonathan Cape Ltd.

Stalin, Joseph. 1954. *Marxism and the National Question*, extracted from *Works*, Vol. 2, 300-81.

Thayil, Jeet. 2012. *Narcopolis*. London: Faber & Faber.

Werbner, Pnina & Tariq Modood. 1997, Eds., *Debating Cultural Hybridity*. London & New York: Zed Books.

12
Reading Globalization*

Globalization at once evokes the image of some business or trade operating in different countries all around the world. The term is usually associated with the expansion of capitalist economy or industry crossing the boundaries of the nation-state, the local, the individual, the society, its history and culture. Obviously, globalization is linked today with the fast-growing processes of digitalization and rapid communication technology. Anthony Giddens, a noted social theorist, thinks that globalization is an expression of an era marked by "the intensification of worldwide relations which link distant localities in such a way that local happenings are shaped by events occurring many miles away and *vice versa*" (1990: 64). In her illuminating book, *A Sociology of Globalization,* Saskia Sassen argues that globalization denotes two distinct things: (1) the emergence of global actors and institutions, such as the World Trade Organization, IMF, financial markets/supermarkets, and the transformation of cosmopolitanism (2007: 5); and (2) the upsurge of transnational activist networks and the replacement of national institutions and standards by international ones. Sassen speaks about a transformation in the relationship between the global and the local, and calls it the "localization of the global" (2007: 4). Globalization, thus, changes the nature of the local, snatching away its assumed isolation, and peripheral status. Similarly, the nation-state no longer remains a closed entity, and the global enters in its processes and practices and the routine

* A lecture delivered at the U.G.C.-Human Resource Development Centre, B.H.U. on 25.3.2017.

life of its inhabitants. Contemporary globalization is, therefore, transnational and translocal in its application and effect.

As noted above, the local and the national are now undergoing a process of transformation because the forces of globalization have become very active today. These forces of globalization have infiltrated into national history, its economy, its language and culture. And all this is happening at a time when the nation, for example India or South Africa, has attained political independence (in the postcolonial times). That's why an Indian scholar, Leela Gandhi, is prompted to remark that "Postcoloniality...is just another name for the globalization of cultures and histories" (1998: 126). In other words, globalization has started the era of transnationalism and trans-culturalism, breaking asunder the boundaries of nation-state and its history and culture.

It would, perhaps, be not wrong to equate 'transnational' with 'international' or with what we term today 'global'. The 'fluid' situation of the nation-state is beautifully articulated by the American poet, Robert Frost, in his famous poem "Mending Wall" where the speaker-persona first says: "Something there is that doesn't love a wall,/ That sends the frozen-ground-swell under it" (1954 & 1967: 235). But later on, the same speaker-persona recalls his father's favourite saying and remarks: "Good fences make good neighbours" (236). No doubt, the speaker-persona's father represents the older generation and his saying may not fit well in the marching times. And then, 'fences' are needed for the individual nation-states, not for a world-order or world-government. It is the world-order that is promoted by the forces of globalization.

Globalization also makes the culture of a country transcultural, and transculturalism is synonymous with 'pluculturalism' or 'multiculturalism'. Homi K. Bhabha calls it 'global cosmopolitanism'. In his Preface to *The Location of Culture* (1994), Bhabha writes thus: "There is a kind of global cosmopolitanism, widely influential now, that configures the planet as a concentric world of national societies extending to global villages...." Such a concept of global 'development' has faith in "the virtually boundless powers of technological innovation and global communications" (xiv). Bhabha maintains that "states that participate in such multicultural multinationalism affirm their commitment to 'diversity', at home and abroad", and this sort of diversity largely consists of "educated economic migrants—computer engineers, medical technicians, and entrepreneurs, rather than refugees, political exiles, or the poor" (xiv). Bhabha naturally envisions in his book a 'world culture' or 'world markets'.

Homi K. Bhabha also suggests that globalization "must always begin at home", and that "a just measure of global progress requires that we first evaluate how globalizing nations deal with 'the difference within'—the problems of diversity and redistribution at the local level, and the rights and representations of minorities in the regional domain" (xv). In this context, Bhabha raises the issue of the status of the Aboriginal peoples of Australia, or that of the Muslims in India, or that of the Negroes in America and Africa. Frequent travels abroad and migrations of nationals to other countries in search of jobs and opportunities broaden the base of globalization. According to Joseph Stiglitz, who was once Senior Vice-President and Chief Economist of the World Bank, the economic solutions to national and international inequality and poverty as practised by the IMF and the World Bank have 'the feel of the colonial ruler' (cited from Bhabha, xvi). Such practices tend to create 'a dual economy in which there are pockets of wealth', and dual economy is not 'a developed economy'. Dual economy makes the poorer society or nation quite vulnerable to the 'culture of conditionality' that is practised under the garb of globalization.

In his Conclusion, Bhabha connects 'globalization' with 'the discourse of modernity' (342, 345-48 etc.), and modernity is linked with 'the present', with 'the here and now', with 'the contemporary'. In one place, he comments thus: "Modernity as a sign of present emerges in that process of splitting, that *lag*, that gives the practice of everyday life its consistency as *being contemporary*" (348). And as the present has the value of a 'sign', modernity is "iterative, a continual questioning of the conditions of existence..." (348).

Pankaj Mishra is also preoccupied with the question of modernity in the era of globalization. In his Foreword to

Temptations of the West (2006), he first mentions his journeys in South and Central Asia—in such countries as India, Pakistan, Afghanistan, Nepal and Tibet—and then outlines the traditional people's efforts in these areas to modernize themselves. He writes herein thus:

> Western ideologies, whether of colonialism, or of communism and globalization, have confronted the countries I visited...with the same challenge: modernize or perish. But the wrenching process of remaking life and society in all their aspects (social, economic, existential) frequently collapses in violence, affecting not just South Asia, but also...the apparently remote and self-contained worlds of the West. ("Forward", n.p.)

So, one of the explicit objectives of globalization, as Pankaj Mishra opines, is the modernization of life and society of the globe. And when this sort of modernization takes place, even an old city like Banaras is transformed by "a rash of fast-food outlets, video-game parlours, and boutiques, the most garish symbols of the entrepreneurial energies unleashed by the liberalization of the Indian economy..." ("Prologue: Banaras: Learning to Read", 4).

The liberalization of the Indian economy was initiated in 1991 by the then Finance Minister, Manmohan Singh (an astute economist who later became the Prime Minister of India for two terms—2004 to 2009 and 2009 to 2014 A.D.). The economic liberalization allowed the ambitious international companies to enter the Indian markets in a spirit of competition. It facilitated such business companies to set up malls and supermarkets, shops of electronic goods and gadgets, buying shares and making huge investments, and also offering jobs to the needy.

Another event of far-reaching significance was the disintegration of the former Soviet Union in 1991. The disintegration of the Soviet Union signalled "the ascent of capitalism both as a formidable developmental alternative and as a world system" (Rajen Harshe, 2013: 4). Prof. Rajen Harshe, an eminent socio-political thinker, is of the view that the current phase of globalization need not be reduced to capitalism, but capitalism has certainly been an agency of globalization. Commenting on capitalism, Prof. Harshe observes:

> Capitalism essentially rests on private/corporate ownership of the means of production, cooperative and conflictual relations between wage labour and capital, socialization of production and privatization of profits that can stimulate the processes of accumulation of capital on the world scale. (2013: 4)

Globalization is "inextricably intertwined with the development of capitalism" (2013: 5). Due to the fast growth of ICT (Information and Communication Technologies) and the explosion of mobile and internet, globalization has facilitated free movements of goods, services, finance, trade, information, people, diseases, and even terrorist activities. Nowadays, the movement of capital has become easier and faster than the movement of labour because of the constraints of nationality or citizenship. The capitalist nations like the USA, UK and many other European countries try to hire labour from developing countries like India at a cheaper rate and make a lot of profits for themselves. That's why a facile question is asked in seminars or conferences whether you are pro-globalization or anti-globalization which clearly indicates your attitude. "Pro-globalization" generally suggests 'pro-rich' and 'anti-globalization' signals 'anti-poor'. Globalization is, thus, linked with capitalism, which is usually characterized by an "uneven development between the sectors, regions, nations, people/classes, and even continents", and uneven development "can fuel social and economic inequalities" (Rajen Harshe, 2013: 5). Homi Bhabha (1994: 177) associates this 'uneven development' with the temporality of modernity' or the 'conditionality of modernity'. Obviously, it cannot be measured in absolute terms, and has a great relevance in the present time.

Globalization definitely promotes consumerist culture, the culture of capitalism and materialism. The consumerist culture is the by-product of a consumer society. In a consumer/consumerist society, as Daniel Miller puts it, "...commodities are increasingly used to express the core values of that society..." (2012: 40). Also, people, come to see, recognize and understand those values through such commodities. To elaborate it, Coca Cola, Pepsi, Denim blue jeans Levi-Strauss, Burger King, McDonald's and Pizza Hut are all signifiers of consumerist culture, for which the

West is so well-known. Paul Hopper (2007) calls it "cultural homogenization as Americanization" (88-90). It is also known as 'McDonaldization' and 'Westernization'. Consumption of goods is the essence of consumerist culture. Daniel Miller makes a clear-cut distinction between 'production' and 'consumption'. He says, "...production, like labour, art and design, is seen as adding to the world. Consumption merely uses the world up" (2012: 41). Both production and consumption are taken care of under globalization; they push to material advancement.

But Wordsworth bewailed the modern man's search for materialism, for money and property, in his famous sonnet "The world is too much with us." Materialism undoubtedly leads to the loss of values, especially moral and spiritual values. It is said the West is materialistic, while the East is spiritualistic, in their outlook upon life.

A recent novel by Aravind Adiga, *The White Tiger* (2008), comes to my mind as an example of modern man's pursuit of materialism and consumerist culture. The action of Balram Halwai is inspired, from the very beginning, by the instincts of the lure of the luce. As a driver, he accompanies his benevolent master, Mr. Ashok, to Delhi where getting a chance, he murders his master for money, and with money he runs away to the deep South, precisely to Bangalore, to become a multi-millionaire.

Globalization being a close ally of capitalism and imperialism is usually associated with modernity and advancement. And as such, it is accompanied with attendant horrors. One of the horrors has already been mentioned, and that is the loss of values in life. Coupled with this horror is the hunt for physical comforts and luxuries. This hunt does not allow modern man to have 'peace of mind, all passion spent', as John Milton puts it. Even T.S. Eliot expresses his deep concern for modern man's want of peace and spiritual pursuit and delivers the message to the world in *The Waste Land* (1922): 'Da Da Da' and 'Shantih Shantih Shantih'.

One of the offshoots of material advancement and capitalism as promoted by globalization is the serious disturbance in ecology. For economic development, too many factories and industries are being set up by business tycoons and industrialists. These factories and industries as well as the large number of vehicular traffic emit out unhygienic gases and smoke. Such emissions of smoke and gases, of petrol and diesel, are proving to be hazardous to human health, creating pollution-borne diseases and ailments across the globe. So much so that the situation has become alarming when the layers of ozone are getting disturbed due to disbalance in Nature. Global warming is an alarming situation, and it has to be controlled immediately for the welfare of mankind. Water storage, stopping soil erosion, planting of trees and plants, checking the unwanted increase of industries: these are some of the measures to restore balance in ecology. Poets like Wordsworth and Coleridge have expressed their deep anxieties over man's loss of love in Nature (see Wordsworth's poems "Tintern Abbey" and "The Education of Nature" particularly for it). Torn Dutt's "Sonnet—The Lotus" and "Our Casuarina Tree" and A.K. Ramanujan's "Ecology" are the other poems stirring in us the love of Nature.

To conclude, globalization is a worldwide phenomenon of our times. It is generally linked with the expansion of capitalist economy or industry operating the world over. Fredric Jameson, who edited the brilliant book, *The Cultures of Globalization* (1998, sixth printing 2004), in collaboration with Masao Miyoshi, mentions four positions of globalization in his paper "Notes on Globalization as a Philosophical Issue": one, there is no such thing as globalization (because there are still nation-states and the national situations); second, there has always been globalization (one needs to go through a book like Eric Wolf's *Europe and the People Without History* (Berkeley, 1982) to form an idea about the neolithic trade routes which have been global in their scope); third, there exists a relationship between globalization and the world market which is the ultimate horizon of capitalism (since the current world networks are only different in degree and not in kind); and fourth, the new multinational stage of capitalism, of which globalization is an intrinsic feature, is associated with 'that thing called postmodernity' (a stage ahead of modernity) (1998 & 2004, 54). Fredric Jameson believes that "globalization is a communicational concept, which alternately masks and transmits cultural or economic meanings" (*Ibid.*, 55).

In his Preface to the book, Jameson defines globalization as "an untotalizable totality which intensifies binary relations between its parts—mostly nations, but also regions and groups, which... continue to articulate themselves on the model of 'national identities'..." (1998 & 2004: xii). Globalization functions in various forms in the realms of the political, the economic, and the cultural. It has its positive and negative points, its advantages and disadvantages. My final reading about globalization is that we should move ahead with it with caution and alertness. Globalization is like a sturdy horse to be trained and tamed for the safety and welfare of mankind.

Works Cited

Adiga, Aravind. 2008. *The White Tiger.* Noida, London, Toronto: HarperCollins Publishers.

Bhabha, Homi K. 1994. *The Location of Culture.* London & New York: Routledge.

Coleridge, S.T. 1941; 7th Indian impr. 1985. "Dejection: An Ode", *Fifteen Poets.* Calcutta: OUP.

Dutt, Toru. 3rd ed. 1994. "Sonnet—The Lotus" and "Our Casuarina Tree", *Ancient Ballads and Legends of Hindustan.* Ed. A.N. Dwivedi. Bareilly: Prakash Book Depot.

Frost, Robert. 1954 & 1967. *The Pocket Book of Modern Verse.* New York: Washington Square Ltd., Inc.

Gandhi, Leela. 1998. *Postcolonial Theory: A Critical Introduction:* New Delhi: OUP.

Giddens, Anthony. 1990. *The Consequences of Modernity:* Cambridge & Malden: Polity Press.

Harshe, Rajen. 2013. "Foreword", *Postcolonial Theory in the Global Age.* Eds. Om Prakash Dwivedi & Martin Kich. Jefferson, North Carolina and London: McFarland & Co. Inc., Publishers.

Hopper, Paul. 2007. *Understanding Cultural Globalization.* Cambridge and Malden: Polity Press.

Jameson, Fredric & Masao Miyoshi. 1998; 6th printing 2004, Eds. *The Cultures of Globalization.* Durham & London: Duke University Press.

Miller, Daniel. 2012. *Consumption and its Consequences.* Cambridge & Malden: Polity Press.

Mishra, Pankaj. 2006. *Temptations of the West.* London: Picador.

Ramanujan, A.K. 1995. "Ecology", *Collected Poems*. New Delhi: OUP.

Sassen, Saskia. 2007. *A Sociology of Globalization*. New York: W.W. Norton.

Wordsworth, William. 1941; 7th Indian impr. 1985. "Tintern Abbey" and "The World is Too Much with Us", *Fifteen Poets*. Calcutta: OUP.

———. 1987; 5th ed. 1998. "Three Years She Drew" or "The Education of Nature", *A Garland of Flowers*. Ed. A.N. Dwivedi. Allahabad: Narayan Publishing House.

Suggestions for Further Reading

Abrams, M.H. *A Glossary of Literary Terms.* New Delhi. Thomson/Heinle, 2006.

Aristotle. *Poetics.* Tr. Humphry House, 1956. Indian rpt. Delhi & Ludhiana, 1970; another tr. Ingram Bywater, *Aristotle on the Art of Poetry.* Oxford, 1920 & 1967.

Arnold, Matthew. *Essays in Criticism, Second Series.* London, 1913.

Atkins, J.W.H. *English Literary Criticism.* 3 Vols. London, 1951. The third volume deals with the seventeenth and eighteenth centuries.

Barry, Peter, *Issues in Contemporary Critical Theory.* London, 1987.

Daiches, David. *Critical Approaches to Literature.* London, 1956.

Dryden, John. *An Essay of Dramatic Poesy.* Ed. Thomas Arnold. London, 1968.

Dwivedi, A.N. *Studies in T.S. Eliot.* 1991; 2nd ed. New Delhi, 2002.

Eastman, Arthur M. *A History of Shakespearean Criticism.* New York, 1968.

Eliot, T.S. *Selected Essays.* London, 1932.

———. *The Use of Poetry and the Use of Criticism.* London, 1933.

———. "The Frontiers of Criticism", *On Poetry and Poets.* London, 1957.

Enright, D.J. and Ernst De Chickera. Eds. *English Critical Texts.* Delhi, 1962 & 1999.

Gondon, David J. *D.H. Lawrence as a Literary Critic.* Yale, 1966.

Henn, T.R. *Longinus and English Criticism.* Cambridge, 1934.

Horace. *Ars Poetica.* Tr. H. Rushton Fairclough. London, 1926.

Leavis, F.R. "Keats", *Revaluation.* London, Oct. 1936.

———. "Arnold as Critic", *Scrutiny,* VII, No. 3, December 1938.

———. *New Bearings in English Poetry.* London, 1961.

Lodge, David. Ed. *Modern Criticism and Theory: A Reader.* London, 1988.

Longinus. *On the Sublime.* Ed. William Smith. London, 1752.

Plato. *The Republic.* Tr. H.D.P. Lee. Harmondshire, U.K., 1955.

Pope, Alexander. *An Essay of Criticism.* London, 1711.

Prasad, B. *An Introduction to English Criticism.* Calcutta & London, 1967.

Pritchard, John Paul. *Criticism in America.* 1956; Indian rpt. Delhi & Ludhiana, 1970.

Richard, I.A. *Principles of Literary Criticism.* 1925; Indian rpt. Delhi (Allied Publishers).

———. *Practical Criticism.* Cambridge, 1929.

———. *Coleridge on Imagination.* London, 1934.

Saintsbury, George. *A History of English Criticism.* Edinburgh, 1911.

Scott-James, R.A. *The Making of Literature.* London, 1930.

———. An Indian edition has been published by Allied Publishers, Ahmedabad & Delhi.

Shawcross, J. Ed. *Biographia Literaria.* Oxford, 1907.

Shipley, Joseph T. *Dictionary of World Literary Terms.* Indian rpt. Delhi, 1993.

Sidney, Sir Philip. *An Apology for Poetry.* Ed. Edward Arber. London, 1595.

Smith, D. Nichol. Ed. *Shakespearean Criticism: 1623-1840.* Oxford, 1916.

Trilling, Lionel. *Matthew Arnold.* New York, 1939 & 1949.

Watson, George, *Literary Critics*. London, 1964.

Wellek, René. *A History of Modern Criticism*. 4 Vols. London, 1955-1966.

Wimsatt, W.K. and Cleanth Brooks. *Literary Criticism: A Short History*. Oxford, 1957.

Wimsatt, W.K. Ed. *Dr. Johnson on Shakespeare*. London, 1969.

Wordsworth, William. *Preface to the Lyrical Ballads*. London, 1800.

Index

A

Abbas, K.A., 91
Abdullah, Mena, 17, 23
Abrams, M.H., 113, 116-19, 126
Achebe, Chinua, 32, 118
Adiga, Aravind, 38, 54, 58-59, 67, 69-70, 75, 118, 139
Aeschylus, 86
Agarwal, Smita, 38, 103, 105, 108-09
Ahmad, Aijaz, 76
Alexander, Meena, 17, 23-25, 103, 105, 107-08, 119
Ali, Agha Shahid, 38
Althusser, Louis, 113, 126
Amanuddin, Syed, 103
Anand, Mulk Raj, 9-10, 16, 35, 38, 54, 59-60
Anandavardhan, 36
Anderson, Benedict, 115, 123
Andrews, C.F., 97
Arnold, Matthew, 67, 113, 126-27
Ashcroft, Bill, 27, 29, 32, 34, 36, 38, 118, 123, 125
Ashvaghosa, 92
Atrey, Mukta, 6
Atwood, Margaret, 35
Aurobindo, Sri, 16, 38, 87-88, 91-92, 96-98
Ayyar, A.S.P., 88
Azad, Maulana Abul Kalam, 39

B

Banerji, Krishna Mohan, 88
Bantock, 48
Barry, Peter, 62, 68, 70, 132
Barthes, Roland, 113, 117, 126, 132
Basham, A.L., 92
Baudrillard, Jean, 62, 65, 68, 116
Bauman, Zygmunt, 122
Beauvoir, Simone de, 4, 7, 119
Becket, Samuel, 117
Bellow, Saul, 30
Bertens, Hans, 74, 129
Bhabha, Homi, 2, 15, 24, 27, 69-70, 76, 114, 123, 138
Bhagat, Chetan, 38
Bhargava, Preeta, 6
Bhasa, 86, 92
Bhatnagar, O.P., 90, 103
Bhatt, Sujata, 17, 23, 37-38, 103, 105, 108-09, 119
Bhatta, S.K., 88
Bhattacharya, Bhabani, 38, 59
Bhavabhuti, 86, 92
Bhoothalingam, Mathuram, 92
Billimoria, J.M., 91
Bissoondath, Neil, 17, 22
Blaise, Clark, 18
Blake, William, 53
Bold, Allan, 52, 60
Bonaparte, Napoleon, 2
Borgaonkar, D.M., 91
Borges, Jorge Luis, 117
Bose, Brinda, 8
Bowers, Faubion, 89
Bowers, Maggie Ann, 84
Brasch, Charles, 35
Brathwaite, Edward Kamau, 33
Brooker, Peter, 70
Brooks, Cleanth, 53
Bruckner, Stephen, 93
Budholia, O.P., 90
Butler, Christopher, 64, 67, 117

C

Carey, Peter, 34
Caster, Angela, 65
Chagla, Hussenali, 91

Chapman, 48
Chattopadhyay, Harindranath, 38, 88-89, 96
Chaucer, Geoffrey, 52
Chaudhari, Nirad, 16
Chitre, Dilip, 103, 107
Clarke, Marcus, 34
Coetzee, J.M., 32
Coleridge, S.T., 43, 46, 50
Conrad, Joseph, 52
Cooper, Brenda, 84
Cowasjee, Saros, 16, 21, 25, 35
Cuddon, J.A., 53, 60, 95
Culler, Jonathan, 77, 114, 115, 119-20
Cummings, E.E., 30
Curnow, A., 35
Currimbhoy, Asif, 87-89, 95

D

Dabydeen, Cyril, 16, 21, 25
Daruwalla, Keki N., 38, 103, 105
Das, Gurcharan, 88-90
Das, Kamala, 3-5, 36-37, 103, 105, 107-09, 119
Dattani, Mahesh, 88, 93
De, Shobha, 56, 119
Deb, Lakhan, 88-91, 95
Derozio, Henry, 37, 96
Derrida, Jacques, 63, 119-20
Desai, Anita, 9, 16, 18, 21, 38, 54-56, 59, 61, 118-19
Desai, Kiran, 16, 18, 38, 67, 77, 119
Desai, S.K., 17, 25
Desani, G.V., 59, 89
Deshpande, Gauri, 38, 107-08
Deshpande, Shashi, 3, 6, 12, 54, 56-57, 59, 61, 77, 119
Dharker, Imtiaz, 105, 108
Dickinson, Emily, 30
Divakaruni, Chitra Bannerjee, 17, 23
Dixon, M., 31
Drabble, Margaret, 118-19
Dryden, John, 47
Dutt, Michael Madhusudan, 16, 88
Dutt, Ram Kinoo, 88
Dutt, Romesh Chunder, 16
Dutt, Toru, 16, 37, 97, 111, 119
Dwivedi, A.N., 38, 107
Dwivedi, O.P., 124

E

Eliot, T.S., 17, 30, 41-49, 52-53, 56, 58, 62, 69, 90, 92, 113, 115-16, 128, 139
Ellman, Mary, 119
Emecheta, Buchi, 9
Euripides, 86
Ezekiel, Nissim, 36, 38, 100, 106

F

Fanon, Frantz, 26, 98, 112-13, 124
Faulkner, William, 116
Forster, E.M., 17, 91
Foucault, Michel, 113, 117, 126
Freud, Sigmund, 66
Frost, Robert, 30, 124, 135
Frye, Northrop, 35
Fuller, Margaret, 119

G

Gandhi, Leela, 125, 135
Gandhi, Mahatma, 31, 39, 90-91
Gardner, Helen, 45
Gay, Paul Du, 99, 128
Geertz, Clifford, 113, 126
Genet, Jean, 119
Ghose, Manmohan, 16
Ghosh, Amitav, 16, 20-21, 25, 77, 117-18
Giddens, Anthony, 134
Gide, Andrè, 115
Glover, Dennis, 35
Godwin, 49
Gokak, V.K., 91
Gokhale, 96
Gordimer, Nadine, 32
Gosse, Sir Edmund, 97

Grace, Patricia, 35
Grieg, Geordie, 80
Gupta, Ashish, 16, 22

H

Habermas, Jurgen, 62, 116
Hall, Stuart, 99, 100, 128
Hariharan, Githa, 3, 6, 38, 77, 119
Harris, Wilson, 33
Harshe, Rajen, 137-38
Hassan, Ihab, 65
Hawthorne, 30
Healey, J.J., 107
Hearne, John, 33
Hemingway, Ernest, 30
Hero, Dilip, 91
Hoggart, Richard, 113, 126
Homer, 98, 115
Hope, A.D., 34
Hopper, Paul, 139
Hoskote, Ranjit, 103, 111
Hough, Graham, 45, 50
Hutcheon, Linda, 62-63, 65-66, 116

I

Ihimaera, Wit, 35
Iyengar, K.R. Srinivasa, 16, 24, 87, 94-95
Iyengar, V.V.S., 92
Iyer, Pico, 17, 23

J

Jagannath, Pt., 36
Jain, Jasbir, 56
Jameson, Fredric, 68, 140
Javanthinathan, R., 91
John, Dryden, 143
Johnson, Barbara, 120
Joshi, Arun, 38, 54-55, 59, 61
Joshi, Sadar, 92
Joyce, James, 52, 65, 115

K

Kafka, Franz, 116
Kailasam, T.P., 88
Kalidas, 86-87, 92, 93
Kannan, Lakshmi, 119
Karnad, Girish, 87-89, 92-93, 95
Keats, John, 44, 50, 54, 102
Keith, A.B., 92, 95
Kirpal, Viney, 6, 57
Kolatkar, Arun, 38, 103, 107
Kortenaar, Neil ten, 72
Krishnamoorthy, K., 36
Krishnaswamy, N., 60, 76
Kulshrestha, Chirantan, 105
Kumar, Shiv K., 38, 103
Kunen, 32
Kuortti, Joel, 124

L

Lahiri, Jhumpa, 17, 23, 38, 77, 130
Lal, P., 36, 38, 102
Lamming, George, 33
Laurence, Margaret, 35
Lawrence, D.H., 119, 144
Lobb, Edward, 45
Longfellow, H.W., 30
Loomba, Ania, 11, 70, 117
Lowell, Robert, 107
Lucy, Niall, 62, 116, 132
Lyotard, Jean-Francois, 62, 64, 116

M

Mahapatra, Jayanta, 38, 103, 105
Mailer, Norman, 119
Mair, G.H., 52
Malgonkar, Manohar, 38, 59, 91
Malik, Keshav, 103
Malouf, David, 34
Mammat, 36
Man, Paul de, 120
Manhire, Bill, 35
Markandaya, Kamala, 3, 16-17, 21, 38, 59, 119
Marx, Karl, 66
Mason, R.A.K., 34

Mathai, Anna Sujatha, 74, 130
Mathew, Ray, 24
Mathur, Smt. K.B., 92
Mattera, Don, 32
Matthiessen, F.O., 45
McLuhan, Marshall, 68
Mehrotra, A.K., 103, 105
Mehta, Gita, 17, 23, 38, 77, 119
Mehta, Ved, 16, 20
Melville, Herman, 30
Miller, Arthur, 30
Miller, Daniel, 138-39
Miller, Henry, 119
Miller, J. Hillis, 120
Millett, Kate, 119
Mill, John Stuart, 119
Milton, John, 139
Mishra, Pankaj, 99, 136-37
Mistry, Rohinton, 16, 22, 35, 38
Miyoshi, Masao, 140-41
Modood, Tariq, 99, 114, 128, 133
Mohanty, Chandra Talpade, 3
Mohanty, Niranjan, 38
Mongia, Padmini, 99
Morrison, Toni, 3, 9
Morton, Stephen, 72
Mtshali, 32
Mukherjee, Neel, 130
Mukherji, Bharati, 3
Muni, Bharata, 36
Munro, Alice, 35

N

Nabokov, Vladimir, 117
Naidu, Sarojini, 16, 37, 96-97, 119
Naik, M.K., 54-55, 87, 91
Naipaul, V.S., 16, 19, 21, 33-34, 38, 59, 118
Nandy, Pritish, 38, 102-03, 105
Narasimhaiah, C.D., 55, 74, 130
Narayan, R.K., 12, 35, 38, 54, 59-60
Nehru, Jawaharlal, 16, 39, 71, 127
Nevinson, Henry, 97
Nietzsche, Friedrich, 66

O

Okri, Ben, 32
O'Neill, Eugene, 30

P

Padmanabhan, Manjula, 88, 93
Pal, Bipin Chandra, 123
Panigrahi, Ramesh P., 93
Parmeswaran, Uma, 16
Parry, Benita, 2, 12
Parthasarathy, R., 36, 38, 105, 107
Patel, Gieve, 103
Patel, Tara, 108
Patke, Rajeev S., 27, 30, 35
Perse, Saint-John, 34
Pickering, Kenneth, 86, 94
Pinto, Jerry, 130-31
Plath, Sylvia, 30, 107
Pope, Alexander, 47
Pound, Ezra, 30, 69, 115
Prasad, Hari Mohan, 35
Premchand, Munshi, 9
Proust, Marcel, 115
Pynchon, Thomas, 65, 117

Q

Quincey, De, 131

R

Rai, Lala Lajpat, 96
Rajan, B., 16-17, 21, 35
Rajan, Tilottama, 16-17, 22
Rakesh, Mohan, 88, 92-93
Ramanujan, A.K., 16-20, 36, 38, 103-05, 140
Rama Sarma, M.V., 91
Rangappa, K.A., 91
Rao, K. Raghavendra, 102
Rao, Raja, 12, 16, 36, 38-39, 54-55, 59, 60
Rau, Santha Rama, 16-17, 21, 25, 91
Ray, Lila, 119
Rayan, Krishna, 36

Roth, Philip, 30
Rothenstein, William, 97
Roy, Arundhati, 3, 7, 9, 11, 13, 23, 38, 54, 57-59, 67, 70, 74, 78, 118-19, 129
Roy, D.D., 92
Roy, Gabrielle, 35
Roy, Raja Rammohan, 2
Rushdie, Salman, 15-16, 18, 21, 25, 27, 38, 59, 63, 67, 69-70, 72, 78, 85, 117-18, 129

S

Sahgal, Nayantara, 3-4, 38, 56, 119
Said, Edward, 2, 15, 24, 76, 117
Sarabhai, Bharati, 88
Sarma, M.V. Rama, 91
Sassen, Saskia, 134
Saussure, 63, 76
Scott, Sir Walter, 53
Selvon, Samuel, 33
Senghor, Leopold, 31
Seth, Vikram, 16, 19, 21
Sexton, Anne, 30, 107
Shakespeare, William, 88, 117
Sharma, Pratap, 91
Shaw, G.B., 91
Shelley, P.B., 51
Shields, Carol, 35
Showalter, Elaine, 118
Silgardo, Melanie, 108
Singh, Charu Sheel, 38
Singh, Manmohan, 137
Sircar, Badal, 88-89, 92-93
Socrates, 100
Sophocles, 86
Souza, Eunice de, 103, 105, 108, 110
Soyinka, Wole, 32, 118
Sozrekashme, Hushmat, 91
Spenser, 45
Spivak, Gayatri Chakravorty, 1, 11, 15, 24, 76, 118
Stalin, Joseph, 123
Stead, Christina, 34
Stein, Gertrude, 115
Stephensen, P.R., 34
Stevens, Wallace, 30, 116
Stiglitz, Joseph, 136
Stopford, 97
Śudrak, 92
Susanne & Lloyd Rudolph, 20
Swinburne, 46

T

Tagore, Rabindranath, 16, 37, 87-88, 96-97
Tendulkar, Vijay, 88-89, 92-93
Thayil, Jeet, 130-31
Thiong'o, Ngugi wa, 118
Thoreau, H.D., 30
Trever, Broadley, 34
Twain, Mark, 80

V

Varma, Monika, 108, 119
Vassanji, M.G., 17, 22
Venugopal, C.V., 90, 95
Vishwanath, 36

W

Walcott, Derek, 34, 118
Walsh, William, 12, 38, 60
Webster, Noah, 30
Werbner, Pnina, 114, 128
White, Patrick, 34
Williams, Dennis, 33
Williams, Raymond, 113, 126
Williams, William Carlos, 30, 116
Wolf, Eric, 140
Wollstonecraft, Mary, 119
Woolf, Virginia, 115, 119
Wordsworth, William, 50
Wright, Judith, 34, 107

Y

Yeats, W.B., 17, 37, 66-67, 97-98, 115